Feminist Antifascism

Feminist Antifascism:
Counterpublics of the Common

Ewa Majewska

VERSO

London • New York

First published by Verso 2021
© Ewa Majewska 2021

This book was written as a part of the project "Early Solidarność and the Black Protests in Theories of Counterpublics and the Subaltern," financed by the Polish National Council of Science, grant no. 2016/23/B/HS2/01338. Some parts of it were made possible by an Institute of Cultural Inquiry (ICI) Berlin research grant, which I was generously offered in 2014–16.

1 3 5 7 9 10 8 6 4 2

Verso
UK: 6 Meard Street, London W1F 0EG
US: 20 Jay Street, Suite 1010, Brooklyn, NY 11201
versobooks.com

Verso is the imprint of New Left Books

ISBN-13: 978-1-83976-116-4
ISBN-13: 978-1-83976-118-8 (US EBK)
ISBN-13: 978-1-83976-117-1 (UK EBK)

British Library Cataloguing in Publication Data
A catalogue record for this book is available from the British Library

Library of Congress Cataloging-in-Publication Data
A catalog record for this book is available from the Library of Congress

Typeset in Minion by Biblichor Ltd, Edinburgh
Printed and bound by CPI Group (UK) Ltd, Croydon CR0 4YY

This book is dedicated to my brave father and to all the girls challenging patriarchal boundaries.

"Order prevails in Warsaw!" "Order prevails in Paris!" "Order prevails in Berlin!" Every half-century, that is what the bulletins from the guardians of "order" proclaim from one center of the world-historic struggle to the next. And the jubilant "victors" fail to notice that any "order" that needs to be regularly maintained through bloody slaughter heads inexorably toward its historic destiny; its own demise.

Rosa Luxemburg, "Order Prevails in Berlin," 1919

Playing the card of naiveté, we wanted to affirm that it was still possible to live and to produce revolutionary subjectivity.

Antonio Negri, "Postscript" to his exchange with Félix Guattari, 2010

CONTENTS

Introduction:
Why Should We Reclaim the Public?

Nevertheless, the desire for being many is nothing to feel bad about.
Sibylle Peters, "On Being Many"

It might seem that the situation in Europe has changed tremendously since the time Rosa Luxemburg wrote her pamphlet "Order Prevails in Berlin." However, while certain things change, much else stays the same. In this book I propose a dismantling of the liberal vision and practice of the public sphere, so as to reclaim the notion of the public and block the growth of fascism. The ideas discussed here amount to a feminist politics of antifascism. However, differently from many books and texts already published on antifascism and the public, this book steps out of the prevailing focus on the West—the cases discussed here as well as some of the conceptual interventions are drawn from the East and South.

I herein discuss theories of counterpublics (those publics or groups that form and organize through mutual recognition of wider public exclusions so as to overcome those exclusions) and the common—the social realm, including humans and their capacities, nature, and the cultural goods in cases of political mobilization originating in Poland, such as the early Solidarność (1980–81) and recent women's protests (2016 onward), for several important reasons. First, while criticism of the one-sidedness and other limitations of "world-focused" vocabulary has been justifiable, the process caused the notion of the Second World to somehow disappear from political maps. This has produced significant theoretical and historical problems, as the majority of today's world could

arguably be classified by this term. Instead, in the name of dismantling dated vocabulary, we entered a world of sharpest distinctions;
while this explained and perhaps combatted the most striking remnants of colonial capitalism, by sweeping the supposedly "developing"
countries off the map, it also made new forms of colonialism and
imperialism invisible.

This book does not offer solutions to the terminology issues, and I
believe some of these problems were resolved in the 1970s by
Immanuel Wallerstein's notions of center, semi-periphery and periphery, however limiting these words might sound today.[1] In his version
of geopolitical theory, the semi-periphery is perhaps the most interesting—and most underutilized—concept. Its supposed dialectic is
always already multiplied, allowing its use even after deconstructing
"world-focused" and other stabilizing notions. The semi-periphery
always tries to become a part of the center and always makes a tre-
mendous effort, sometimes particularly brutally, to cut any of its
associations with the periphery. It is always lured into more prestigious positions and never fully allowed its honors. Poland was listed
as one such country by Wallerstein back in the 1970s, and—as this
book in many ways shows—has kept its in-between position, with all
the consequences of such situatedness. It will never be fully Western;
however, it is in many ways not South, North or East, either. It
constantly struggles to become "more Western." And the impossibility
of accomplishing such a transition is part of the bargain. Perhaps we
will always be Europe's "class B" citizens, desperately trying to join
the best in the club while disregarding and abusing all those even
weaker in the region and globally.

The accuracy of this description somehow proves that the global
dynamics did not fully erase the binary oppositions—while it might
shift the power distribution in the world, it did not erase its central
mechanisms. My version of postcolonialism adapted here allows for
dismantling the hidden presumptions of any notion of globalization;
however, it does not submit to the cruel optimism of some anticol-
onial efforts, in which the polishing of the geopolitical vocabulary
tacitly replaced the far more complex struggle for recognition. Such
changes, as needed as they truly are, never are enough.

The structure of this book is simple. The introduction shares insights as to the book's context and subsequent content. I then discuss the beginnings of Solidarność as an example of the counterpublics of the common and also as a vibrant utopia. Solidarność (Solidarity) was an independent workers' union established in August 1980 after a two-week strike initiated by workers of the shipyard of Gdańsk; they were joined, in solidarity (hence the name), by some 700,000 workers from 700 other workplaces across the country—including the majority of Poland's key workplaces—so it was in fact a general strike. In the process of negotiating with the then-communist Polish government, the independent workers' union, Solidarność, was registered and by March 1981 it counted 10 million official members. However, Poland's process of democratic reform was stopped by the sudden introduction of the martial state on December 13, 1981.* In my analysis, I offer a critique of Jürgen Habermas's theory of the public sphere, and liberal political theory more generally, as being based on fundamental exclusions and stabilizing them. The work of Lauren Berlant, particularly her concept of cruel optimism, is important to capture our current disappointment with the conservative line of today's Solidarność, and it also helps to emphasize its optimistic beginnings.

Chapter 2 discusses women and LGBTQ+ persons in the public sphere as well as the notion of feminist counterpublics, coined by Nancy Fraser. Through analyzing Zorka Wollny's artwork, I show the impossibility of women's political agency in male-dominated politics. Later in this chapter, I discuss the recent women's protests in Poland, and globally, as examples of feminist counterpublics. Social reproduction theory is depicted as an important theoretical shift within

---

* When I discuss Solidarność in this book, I only mean its first period of existence, between August 1980 and December 13, 1981, when the union was delegalized and repression followed. Any mentions of today's Solidarność are highlighted. In 1989, though, the situation changed, leading to the first democratic election in former East Europe on July 4, 1989, and further changes in Poland and the region, including the second legalization of Solidarność and its later atrophy to the position of the current conservative government's fierce servant.

feminism, one that clearly indicates that reproductive rights or gender-based violence are not merely problems of certain conveniently essentialized and exoticized groups, but are of general social importance. I also consider the topic of academia and the feminist counter publics within it, as we tend to see university-based feminism mainly as theory. In this discussion, I emphasize the internationalism of the feminist movement, as well as the role of new media, for processes of solidarity networks and feminist political agency globally.

This book is rooted in theory as well as in social activism. I discuss the feminist counterpublics in academia in Chapter 2 partly to show how deeply universities need change and partly to depict struggles I know firsthand. The book overall aims to continue the early Frankfurt School's legacy of theory that intervenes and is rooted in current struggles. Such books are almost absent in Poland, however, where "a blanketing snow [has] begun to drift over the radical history," as Adrienne Rich once wrote about the United States.[2] This text can also be seen as an exercise in Marxist-feminist thought, although post-structuralist strategies are also applied.

Chapter 3 discusses the various layers of the making of counter publics of the common, based on examples from Poland. These include the early Solidarność and recent women's protests, often referenced as the Black Protests due to the black clothing worn by protestors and featured on social media. I also consider the women's strike in Poland, which took place on October 3, 2016, and was expanded in subsequent months to the International Women's Strike by women in Poland and some seventy countries. The most important topics addressed by these women's protests include reproductive rights and violence against women, which includes sexual harassment at work, a topic of the huge campaign involving #MeToo. This hybrid of issues is transversal at its core, and this is what makes the feminist counterpublics so fascinating and effective. The women's protests in Poland and globally activated several layers of society, involving street demonstrations, actions on social media, artistic work, strikes, a refusal to fulfill housework duties, artistic actions, legal investigations and new law proposals. This means that the debate between reformism and revolution was somehow absent—everybody was protesting in ways they found most convincing and available.

In Chapter 3, I briefly discuss the counterpublics of the common.* Moving between the theories of the common, as conceptualized by Antonio Negri and Michael Hardt, and the proletarian and feminist counterpublics of Alexander Kluge, Oskar Negt, and Nancy Fraser, respectively, I argue for a new notion of the intersection of the supposedly incompatible theoretical traditions of Spinozean Marxism and critical theory.[3] Such work was to some extent inspired by the proposition of "institutions of the commons" discussed by Gerald Raunig.[4]

In Chapter 4, I offer notes on weak resistance, the unheroic and common forms of protest and persistence that led to a redefinition of the most general notions of political agency in feminist and minoritarian ways. The concept of weak resistance was coined during my 2014–16 research work at the ICI Berlin, and it was first publicly outlined in the conference "Weak Resistance," which we organized at the Institute with Rosa Barotsi and Walid El-Houri in 2015. Later, I worked on several aspects of "weakness" on my own, including articles and presentations on the weak avant-garde as well as on more general studies of weak resistance as an alternative to the predominantly straight and masculine notions of heroic activism dominating our political imaginary. The obvious inspiration for such a reconceptualization of political agency is the work of Walter Benjamin and his idea of "weak messianism," understood as a pact between generations of the oppressed and excluded as a (methodological and political) duty of historical materialism. My work is also inspired by the seminal essay of Václav Havel, Czech dissident and later president of the

---

* By "the common," I mean the social realm, including humans and their intellectual and affective capacities, embodied; nature, including animals, plants and what used to be called "resources"; and the cultural goods produced by humans. The concept comes from the work of Antonio Negri and Michael Hardt, particularly *Commonwealth*, and differs substantially from "the commons," which only encompass the products of culture and those parts of nature which are used as "resources." See M. Hardt and A. Negri, *Commonwealth*, Cambridge: MIT University Press, 2009.

Czech Republic, namely *The Power of the Powerless*, which considers prospects of ordinary, everyday resistance. Such weak resistance can be seen as the agency fueling counterpublics of the common.

The closing summary asserts that contemporary global feminism is the most important antifascist struggle, arguing for a major shift in political theory that still separates feminism as some "other politics" rather than situating it at the core of today's political struggles—as should be the case, given the efficiency, internationalism and numbers of those involved in feminism today. This book aims to change this classic yet dated tendency, and it thus argues not only for "embracing feminism," which is already a given in progressive political theory and struggles, but also to see it as the central political force resisting fascism as well as one shaping the alternatives to such a brutal world order in various ways and regions.

This book was written in Warsaw, a city almost entirely destroyed by the fascists during World War II. All streets in the city center have information about the borders of the Jewish Ghetto and the numbers of people killed on various corners and areas. This is a city the Nazis occupied for five long years and then had to surrender. Back in 1939, they also had plans to change this vibrant capital—inhabited by approximately 1 million people of multiple ethnic and cultural backgrounds, including the largest population of Jews in Europe—into a labor camp of merely 10,000 slave workers.[5] Living in this city builds a sense of responsibility and makes Benjamin's words about weak messianism particularly tangible, not in a mystical sense, but quite concretely—some of the WWII survivors are still alive, and it just seems wrong to disappoint them and allow fascism to come back here after all these years.

Warsaw is also a city of wild reprivatization, which—as Joanna Kusiak bravely shows in her research about the current urban politics—constitutes a form of primitive accumulation of capital after 1989 and was necessary for the transition toward neoliberal capitalism.[6] She writes about "at least 10,000 families" displaced in Warsaw alone during this process. This can roughly be translated into 40,000 people who were deprived of their households in the holy name of private property, the divine object of the neoliberal order. The Warsaw movement against the uncontrolled reprivatization of apartments and entire buildings was formed by people evicted from their homes, sometimes under false claims made by lawyers through forged testimonies. They have been joined by grassroots activists like Jan Śpiewak, who now faces more than twenty court cases for his involvement, and politicians who include Piotr Ikonowicz—who used his privileged position as the socialist Member of Parliament to highlight the topic in the media while actively preventing evictions in direct actions—and Anna Grodzka, Poland's first transgender MP, who focused on the issue of homelessness and reprivatization during her term. It also involves young politicians, squatters from the Syrena Collective, and the Warsaw-based Stowarzyszenie Lokatorów (Association of Tenants). Since city hall has been known to accept illegitimate claims, the legal situation is messy and demands clarification. Poland does not have a single law organizing such property claims, as do other countries in the region. Opposing these often illegal and always cruel evictions sometimes involves actual blockades. The legal claims of those threatened by evictions are backed by the constitutional right to shelter—particularly important as Poland is a country where the temperature falls below zero degrees Celsius for several months every year.

We could, of course, go back to the times when the state did not regulate housing, and we remember from postwar experience, books, and documentaries what that meant.[7] Instead of doing this, we need an understanding of housing as the common—as not just a right, but a collective responsibility—and the counterpublics uniting those excluded and their supporters help to provide a vision and a practice of such politics. We cannot only understand housing as a private matter, as most Aristotelians or Habermasians would, or only as a matter of institutional decisions. We need to understand the right to housing as a threefold, transversal right that is built of needs, laws and responsibilities—of all society, not merely its institutions or isolated social activists. Every winter, at least fifty people freeze to death in Poland. Since 1989, Warsaw has become a city where everyone is fixated on buying and owning their flat. The number of city-owned apartments is the lowest among European capitals and dropping; the average tenant spends 70 percent of their salary on rent. We must imagine the public institutions, like city hall, following another agenda and transitioning toward the common, investing in housing for the people and not merely for profit.

These facts are perhaps sufficient inspiration for my project of reclaiming the public sphere. However, as the city and state institutions are corrupt—not merely in the most rudimentary sense of the word, but also more metaphorically—they have ceased defending the public interest and succumbed to the holy notion of private property, the need to redefine what is public is a priority. As provided in Negri and Hardt's theory, which includes the notion of the common as a third option between the private (as in ownership, but also intimate) and the public (understood as merely private expanded to the dignity of an institution), it is inspiring to see the extent to which such a notion can be applied in this extravagant, semi-peripheral context, where some institutions are still public in a good sense. It also seems compelling to reclaim the concept of the public sphere—for long decades, even centuries, hijacked by liberals mainly to defend the exclusivity of politics and separation of the private sphere from it. In this way, the theories of counterpublics I mentioned provide a good starting point as well. However, as they more or less ignore the affective composition of social struggles and do not offer a vision of the public beyond institutions as we know them, an effort to merge their strengths with Negri and Hardt's propositions seems interesting and perhaps useful, maybe as a failure we all need to learn from and perhaps as a proposition of a new theoretical paradigm. The idea of weak resistance appears as a necessary element of such an intersection.

Some argue that theory should be kept apart from practice to provide a reflexive distance, one that separates the intellect from actions and needs. Such a perspective found a very important proponent in Hannah Arendt, and has been extended by Judith Butler. However, another option, chosen by Marx and the Frankfurt School, was to root theory *in* social struggles, assuming, somewhat in Hegel's style, that to be modern means to engage with the entire historical process, including the parts of it unfolding now, perhaps most importantly. While I have some sympathy toward reflexive distance, I tend to think that as it has a very strong tendency to transform into a reactionary legitimization of the status quo, it should be handled carefully and perhaps with necessary interruptions. In what follows, I discuss the clashes between Jean Baudrillard and Susan Sontag as an unmediated example of such division, and I also analyze discussions between Jodi Dean versus Antonio Negri and Michael Hardt as a far more nuanced version of such disputes.

Critical theory undermines the liberal model of the public sphere, still pertinent in public debates and recently used as a form of opposition to fascist tendencies in contemporary politics. Today, liberal opposition in Poland and in other countries, especially the United States, uses the charge of fascism against ultraconservative governments. This argument may be correct, but the criticism behind it is shallow. It is arguably not critical enough, if by critical we mean the search for conditions of possibility. Ritualistic comparisons of Kaczyński or Trump to Hitler seem largely artificial when performed by members of the economic and cultural establishment, the very people responsible for the perpetuation of what Naomi Klein has termed "the shock doctrine"—neoliberalism, with its economic and military violence all over the globe. This is the reason so many people today demand a move toward the left, socialism, communism or social democracy.

In this book, this demand is not only an inspiration, but I also try to find a way for political theory and practice to overcome the limitations and disbelief imposed after the supposed "collapse of communism" in 1989. This collapse and what followed it is here presented as the "defeat of solidarity," as David Ost describes it in his own book on the topic. There is much in this account with which I agree—but I have a different perspective on the failed promises of Solidarność. I do not think the problem stemmed mainly from the attack on elites by the workers.[8] The workers were to a large extent betrayed by cultural elites, and this is very well-established and accepted, not only in the adoption of hard-line neoliberal capitalism in Poland after 1989, but also in the accounts of Solidarność produced by the intelligentsia since the early 1980s. I believe Solidarność was not misogynist in its early days, just as it was not anticommunist. In 1980, Solidarność was built to fulfill the socialist premises of state communism in an egalitarian way, without privileging the members of the ruling party.

We on the left might want to be better prepared to oppose the dark forces of fascism in contemporary politics, as it is unlikely that using one elitism (liberal) against another (conservative) will suffice. As I aim to show, the theories and practices of counterpublics provide much more egalitarian models of political togetherness in resistance than the liberal ideology of the exclusive public sphere. Counterpublics are rooted in the embodied, lived experiences of heterogeneous groups and societies as well as in their production. They are not merely inclusive but hybrid, practicing solidarity rather than support. The distinction between solidarity and support is perhaps best explained in bell hooks' *Feminist Theory: From Margin to Center.* She observes that even those who have experienced the worst oppression or abuse are always sharing their experiences, strategies and knowledge with those who help them. This exchange is never just one-directional; it moves both ways. For example, victims of violence share their strategies of survival and recovery with those who are with them in these hard situations, providing patterns of avoiding and resisting violence and trauma for others.[9] It therefore seems particularly unjust to see relations of "support" typically depicted as one-sided. A more accurate notion of solidarity encompasses mutuality and being together, as they better describe the social relations among the oppressed.

My analysis of the public sphere and counterpublics partly draws on my research and academic work, and it is also rooted in lived experience by way of personal memories of activism and resistance. Many of these experiences can be seen as executing the "right to the city," as Henri Lefebvre puts it, particularly important for the experience of the public in a clash with the common.[10] One such recollection comes from events that took place around the year 2000, involving techno parties we held in a space in one of the bridges over the Vistula river in Warsaw. Today these events are sometimes "discovered" by curators of modern art museums while they are documenting techno cultures. They also feature in commentaries on Warsaw's underground music scene. Still other times, these events are recalled nostalgically at parties and demonstrations.[11] Some of us were involved in a post-situationist group practicing intense psycho-geography; others were anarchists, music students or both. Someone spotted a huge space in one of the bridges over the Vistula, conveniently distanced from any inhabited buildings. Made of concrete and steel, it sat right on the riverbank. A perfect venue for a rave/drum and bass party. Someone said they knew some DJs; someone else offered to buy enough beer to make it a party. The only thing still missing was the advertising—posters for wheatpasting and a public invite on the local independent radio station. There was also the small matter of borrowing a sound system along with begging help from electricians to install it. We had a party to make. On the day of the first of those "under-the-bridge parties," a police car stopped right out front. A cop came in and asked politely, "Who is the boss of all this?!" We were in the middle of setting up. We looked at each other and, in a flash, someone answered without missing a beat, "He'll be back in thirty minutes." The policeman smiled and said, "I'll be back then, too." But he never returned. And the party went on, with almost a thousand happy people dancing all night without any permit or property over the site. This was repeated some six times, until some local mafia discovered the place, and we all understood that the happy days were over.

There was another tense moment when the older guys who were renting us the sound system asked, "Do you have any permits to do this?" We said, "Sadly, no." "Okay," they said. "Give us a minute." A while later, they came back and said, "Well, we also squatted some ten years ago. We'll stay with you." This was a swift and surprising revelation. We knew this was going to work—and it did. The fact that no one got hurt or drowned in the river is a miracle. The space was rough, with metal parts protruding from the concrete. The river was just meters away. So much could have gone wrong but nothing did. The police never came back, not that night nor on any other. We had our six or seven parties, and it seemed like we could occupy at least a small part of the city. Later, when I studied the public sphere and counterpublics, this event always came to mind. For one of the parties, someone forgot to bring the stamp to mark the hands of those who had gained admission. While waiting for her, I made an alternative mark by writing a sentence from Heraclitus on their forearms with a pen. *"Aión país esti paízon, paídos he basileíe"*—eternity is a playing child, the kingdom is the child's own. Luckily the stamp arrived after an hour or so; any later and I would have drowned in metaphysics. But I still remember watching the river and sensing that no one would even attempt to copy this sentence, especially if I wrote it in Greek, which I did, some seventy times in a row. This situation is a very good example of repetitive, mundane and simultaneously also necessary reproductive labor. It is far less demanding than housework, yet I was tired of it soon enough and yet had to continue. This example demonstrates the need for contingency as an element of every social mobilization—but it also gives a sense of what I will call "fluid modernity," following Zygmunt Bauman. We, the suddenly precarious of Europe's East, were also using the privilege of rather luxurious knowledge in the service of events directed against the system.

Guy Debord's *The Society of the Spectacle* captures the mechanisms of alienation in a clever glimpse into yet another definition of ideology: as a totality of images and the ways in which they mediate relations between humans, eventually replacing any direct social relations. Debord's critique of commodification, however, seems to stop short of demanding an unmediated society. This chafes against his compelling claim for the critical ability to dismantle the spectacle and to create a human environment according to desires. The demand of *sous les pavés, la plage*, which we carried around Warsaw in 1998, clearly connotes the May of 1968 in the streets of Paris and other European cities.* The desire to shape our lives in opposition to the capitalist logic of late postmodernity was always connected—somewhat against the grain of Debord's small groups of the political avant-garde—to the making of large social movements and debates for those excluded, who usually appear as unidentified and neglected

---

* *Sous les pavés, la plage* is famous French slogan from May 1968, meaning "under the pavement, a beach." See also: G. Debord, *The Society of the Spectacle*, trans. D. Nicholson-Smith, New York: Zone Books, 1994.

"masses." The tension—between a sharp, small group *detourning* the advertisements and political slogans or practicing psychogeography and the efforts to build genuinely democratic, massive forms of political expression, such as large political parties, demonstrations, Indymedia and the alter-globalization movement, for example—is a fruitful one. In the times of the rise and mass popularity of fascist politics, we on the left should also consider effective ways of becoming many.

Since 1990, a hard version of capitalism has been imposed in Poland. Naomi Klein's book *The Shock Doctrine* provides a great summary of the neoliberal procedures mercilessly implemented in the already poor society after 1989. In the late 1990s, I became a leftist-feminist queer scholar, which makes me a persona non grata in the largely anti-Marxist, often prejudiced and sexist Polish academe. Much has changed since I did my PhD, when some of the professors would scream during the departmental meetings that "feminist doctorates will be defended over our dead bodies!" Today they do not need such exclamations; the neoliberal system of precarized academia allows them to hire and fire scholars as they please, without entering any political discussion. Feminist scholars today are often pushed away from teaching because of their opinions. Mobbing and public corrections are used to intimidate us out of teaching our methodologies and research; we are threatened with firing, demotion or are simply neglected. Sometimes this comes unexpectedly, from colleagues who are supposedly progressive. While this shaming, bullying and harassment makes the atmosphere unbearable, it is even worse when financial precarity and mobbing are (often) used as forms of departmental management. This was made possible by the neoliberal economic transition of the 1990s, when former members of the independent workers' union, Solidarność, together with a majority of members of the former Communist party, transformed belonging to a union into a shame or a threat and demands for economic equality into unwelcomed radicalism. This is the climate in which I grew up, in a country where entire swathes of society were forced into poverty while leftist politics were denied space in political debates. Obviously, this made of me a rather monstrous subject, learning from history without obedience to current fashions and therefore crossing the lines of what is currently interesting in an effort to practice history critically—with a modern, self-reflexive twist.

Today, much is being said about the rise of fascism. There is talk of how multiple political parties, organizations and groups are copying and reinventing ultra-right politics; there is also talk of the more or less silent response from the liberal center, sometimes correctly called "radical" since it eradicates the left, thus liquidating any critique of neoliberal injustices other than of the ultra-right.[12] Here in Poland, we have a government that came to power around 2015 largely thanks to their racist anti-immigration position. They were spreading spurious statements—for instance, connecting recent epidemics with refugees—and the conservative parties' candidates copied the contagion narratives used by the Nazis against the Jews in the 1930s. Poland's current government also astonished everyone in 2017 by trying to pass a law banning research and publications on "Polish participation in the crimes of the Holocaust," which was in fact a law restricting research on an important and definitely understudied part of Nazi crimes and those who perpetrated them. Although the law was finally changed and its most outrageous parts were erased, shame still covers Poland's engagement with international politics, as this attempted revisionism was only tempered due to official protest by politicians from Israel, the United States, Germany and the rest of the European Union. Poland's conservative government is also promoting a valorous vision of Poland's past, emphasizing its (rare) military victories and fetishizing the (more common) failures, thus imposing on the population a heroic, martyrological model of citizenship and political agency.

Such heroism is also forced on women via limitations on access to contraceptives, abortion and reproductive health strategies. This is also promoted by the image of the (self-sacrificing) Polish mother, who combines a patriotic sense of reproductive obligation with a resignation from career and political ambition. This symmetry of heroic subjective formations, binary in their gender roles, forces men to hate "Others" and to build brotherly structures focused on "enemies," while enforced reproduction, regardless of choices or costs, makes a necropolitical pact of citizenship in such a state of exception.[13] The doctrine of absolute sovereignty, which makes the law, yet is itself beyond its regulations, has early modern roots in Jean Bodin's theory and earlier in ancient Rome. In the twentieth century, it was expanded by Carl Schmitt, the philosopher of law, whose work was central in the transition of the German legal system during the rise of the Third Reich. The exceptionality organizes the absolute rulers, as well as those who occupy the position of the "enemy," who are to be stripped of all rights, property, position, and eventually— also life. In the more recent theory of the state of exception offered by Giorgio Agamben, the place of the *homo sacer*—the figure who is beyond the law and in many ways reminiscent of Schmitt's "enemy"— is occupied by refugees. In this book I often discuss women and LGBTQ+ people as those pushed into such a state of exceptionality.[14]

As I argue in Chapter 2, this enforced reproductive subordination is the reason we should see the Polish government's current state of exception as gendered biopolitical rule and thus also see feminism as a core position against fascism. This "identity politics of heroism" is a backlash, a repressive response to the heritage of 1968, and it should be seen as one based on a very complex vision of recognition, one that is not gained by labor but by facing the risk of death. Indeed, I believe we are witnessing perhaps the most anti-Marxist climax ever in this current heroic subject formation, one in which many of us must face death, whether actual (as happens more often to women) or symbolic (involving far more men, if we look at contemporary fascist groups). Neoliberal capitalism teaches us that only profit matters—and thus any strategy, even the fascist one, seems like the one to follow.

In this general state of exception, the juridical sector is almost fully subordinated to the executive and the Constitutional Court practically deactivated by contradicting laws. This imposition of heroic subjectivity seems like a natural element in exercising the Schmittian state of exception. After decades of neoliberal economic transformation, the time has come for restructuring biopolitical power into a fascist state format. Threatened by poverty or living in it already, the majority of Poland's population cannot count on any support other than familial. The triad—state, church and family—is at the heart of a fascist vision of the state run as a paterfamilias rather than by demo-cratically chosen and controlled forces. This is a repetition of the 1930s ideology to a much greater extent than most theorists and politicians are willing to admit. It is therefore necessary, not just a theoretical choice, to approach these transformations as they are: driven by the old Schmittian doctrine, which demands that the sover-eign should always be beyond the law, even while making it.[15]

It could, however, be interesting and inspiring to revise the classi-cal response to Schmitt. I am thinking of that offered by Walter Benjamin, not just in his *Theses on the Philosophy of History* but also in his other writings on proletarian aesthetics and reproduction. It is there that we find the most thrilling defenses of the ordinary and common against elitist trends in culture, as well as the lived experi-ence more generally of several generations.[16] The notion of weak messianism was only briefly mentioned by Benjamin in his *Theses*, where he wrote about a pact between the past, contemporary and future generations, one that consists of giving account, a task of the historical materialist. This idea was later elaborated by Jacques Derrida in *Specters of Marx*; it also inspired the sudden turn toward dialectics in other poststructuralist theories, including Gianni Vattimo's *Weak Thought*. I reference them here as inspirations for the idea of "weak resistance."[17]

There is an important aspect of Benjamin's weak messianism that is particularly relevant to the contemporary rise of fascism—the aforementioned "pact" between generations. Living in Warsaw, I walk the streets, which sometimes directly commemorate fascism's victims on their pavements. There is a line marking the wall of the Warsaw Jewish Ghetto as well as plaques and monuments paying tribute to people murdered by fascists. When I encounter these monuments, I wonder how far we've progressed from there. Raised and educated in communist Poland, I was taught that fascism would "never again" come back. My history teacher had this habit of repeating the Polish word "simply" (*po prostu*) and as she was a devoted antifascist, she would sometimes scream "Remember, children, Hitler was a psycho-simply-path" (*Hitler był psycho, po prostu, patą*). I wonder whether kids today also have this kind of passionate antifascist education—or whether they are learning some alternative history lessons in which society has to be structured according to the hierarchy established by some *ubermensch*. The most ironic paradox of this revival of the cultural hegemony of the right wing, at least in schools, historical politics and museums—which are, by the way, enough to shape the mindset of entire generations, especially if you add churches and religious lessons—is that under German fascism, Jews were stripped of humanity, but Poles were *untermenschen*, the "under-humans" who were mainly useful as slaves. Therefore, the marches of semi-military Polish youth wearing dark brown clothes, sometimes decorated with fascist symbols, not only constitute a repetition of the symbolism that led to the Holocaust, but they also prove the ignorance of those contemporary followers of Nazi politics.

In this politics, the place of women is definitely in the home. Although politicians such as Marine Le Pen are currently shifting their ultra-right political parties away from the misogynist traditions of the right, in Poland it is very clear that women have other duties than men and they should stick to them. It is, however, also very clear that both men and women should follow the heroic pattern of citizenship, which means fighting for their homeland and giving birth regardless of the risks. Since the current Polish government limits access to prenatal health care, contraceptives and abortions, they clearly force on women a heroism that is akin to that attributed to men who have died for their homeland in military battles. The paradox, however, is that most women choose abortion anyway—at least, this is the claim of feminist organizations, who indicate that the number of abortions in Poland exceeds 100,000 per year, regardless of whether women are heroic patriots or feminists. They can access it in Poland or abroad; it is just a question of money. Alongside this, groups of contemporary nationalists pressure each other to display excessive heroism in the streets, while marching in neo-Nazi demonstrations or beating up refugees. They have few other occasions to prove their heroic devotion to their homeland and hence are condemned to small-scale excesses of heroism while humiliating or beating up women, refugees, queer people or leftist politicians. It is important to see the symmetry between the versions of masculine and feminine heroism imposed on us today as political ideology.

The idea of "weak resistance" offers a framework that dismantles the heroic models of identity. The examples of heroism imposed in Poland—macho patriotism and heroic motherhood—are perhaps the most drastic. However, there are other, weaker demands based on the heroic vision of politics, some of them on the left, that require dismantling or at least recomposing due to their elitist, conservative content. For instance, ignoring ordinary, daily forms of resistance and focusing on the most spectacular is one of the ways that the patriarchal, white, privileged and heteronormative perspective survives. While women struggle against masculine domination on every front of their lives for decades, it still seems easier to attribute "politics" or "resistance" to a twenty-year-old man who went to a demonstration or two. This is just wrong. And I do not say it against men in their twenties, going to demonstrations—please do not take my comments personally. Rather, think about all those who struggle for decades, resisting patriarchal, racist, heteronormative capitalism every day. Ain't that politics?

I once directly responded to a very young man who, in a public discussion, expressed his fatigue and disappointment after a year of activism. Some participants of this gathering just looked at me, whose fatigue and disappointment had some twenty-five years to grow, and they smiled. I smiled too, as there is no sense in determining when we are allowed to feel despair—it can happen anytime, and rightly so, as it is natural under conditions of precarized labor, forced nomadism and gender discrimination, just to mention a few problems we all currently face. This situation was very familiar to Rosa Luxemburg, and there are many moments in her pamphlets and correspondence dedicated to this struggle with despair and resignation. Luxemburg, however, contrary to the recently popular "melancholy on the left," rightly criticized by Wendy Brown, among others, suggested that despair is a feeling only available to those free of daily struggle against oppression. Those who have to fight on a daily basis get used to failures and go further. It is not about feelings, though. Luxemburg was a very affective person; she did not advocate the abolition of feeling. What she meant, however, was that failure is inevitable, and it should be experienced as a part of the process of building alternatives to capitalism, not as proof of the futility of such efforts. Genuine social change might not happen all at once; it starts with failures, and it will most certainly be attacked, as was Luxemburg herself. Loralea Michaelis discusses Luxemburg's take on the issue of failure and disappointment, claiming: "The philosophy of history which Luxemburg absorbed from Marx, notably through the Eighteenth Brumaire, prophesies the ultimate victory of socialism but ordains that the actual events and experiences through which this victory is prepared will consist in catastrophes rather than conquests."[18] In her meticulous analysis of Luxemburg's correspondence and political texts, Michaelis argues for what I would call an appreciation of weakness and failure as elements of the historical process of making change. Her historical materialism is therefore an embodied, contextualized one, one with feelings, even while some of those feelings should be worked upon. I believe this argument is crucial in the transition from patriarchal to feminist political theory, and it constitutes an important part of this book. The recent women's protests, I argue, are bringing this insight concerning embodiment and context into political praxis. In the discussion with the tired young man, we spoke about the dialectics of historical process and how it also consists of rehearsals and failures, including our own fatigue or despair. The issue, then, is not how to erase this, as has been done by the brave heroes of past resistances, but how to embrace it in ways that allow further development. In this discussion I also realized that I did not become a resentful, angry frog, which was a small yet satisfying thought.

This book is an effort to build leftist, feminist political theory. The central notions I use—counterpublics, weak resistance and feminism—are not merely inclusive, they are hybrid, and in each of them is taken for granted the possibility of not being a man or a woman but someone of the multiplicity of other genders. I do use the words "woman" and "women" in their social sense, as denominators of those people who assume "feminine" roles, were socialized accordingly and are discriminated against accordingly. If I say less about

LGBTQ+ communities, it is not because of essentialism but instead because of the main examples of social mobilizations discussed here, of which one was workerist and the other mainly focused on reproductive rights. However, in Chapter 2, I move between "women" and "women and LGBTQ+ persons," trying to embrace a wide and hybrid spectrum of embodied experiences we all have in the context of sexuality and gender. I obviously reject any effort to stabilize gender-normative discourse and, as much as possible, try to avoid claims that might sound essentializing.

As many feminist authors have argued before me—and I directly refer to Carole Pateman here, as she also worked on the workers' movement and on feminist political theory—what we know as the social contract is in fact a fraternal political structure, preserving masculinity as the hegemonic version of subjectivity and keeping the majority of women and LGBTQ+ persons away from core positions within the structures of power. Pateman argues that liberal politics functions as a republic of brothers, in which absolute paternal power is not erased but instead transformed into the power of men over women.[19] Using the idea of patriarchy as a theoretical tool, Pateman's theory might today sound essentialist, especially if we consider the queer politics and theory as well as the growing rejection of binary gender roles in contemporary societies. However, many of our societies are shaped according to what we know as patriarchy. Reproductive labor is still widely perceived as secondary to waged labor, and therefore it is also paid and respected much less than what passes as "production." In Pateman's argument, violence against women figures centrally, and given the statistics—which in Europe and, interestingly, in Poland and in Sweden alike, show that some 30 percent of women are victims of domestic violence—this centrality seems perfectly justified.[20] Thus our habit of perceiving the public sphere as some valley of happiness in which we immerse ourselves in wisdom and common topics should be replaced by another, more accurate vision, one in which the majority of societies do not even allow access to true public debate. Furthermore, those who enter it from outside of its elitist core pay a very harsh price. The names of Martin Luther King Jr., Malcolm X, Stephen Biko,

Rosa Luxemburg, Olympie de Gouges, Nelson Mandela, Lech Wałęsa, Angela Davis, Emma Goldman, to some extent my father, Henryk Majewski, and so many others, globally, make this point very clear.

I hope that the examples of social mobilization I chose to discuss here and the theoretical contexts of counterpublics, the common and weak resistance will collectively contribute to an antifascist politics, of which we are so very much in need today. If you disagree, though, perhaps the analysis offered here will be the failure to inspire better propositions. Regardless, we all need to work against fascism, in all contexts in which we work and live. Perhaps there is an eight-year-old girl somewhere who is desperately willing to kick some patriarchal, neo-Nazi ass. This book was written for her.

1

Revisiting "Solidarity": Counterpublics, Utopia and the Common

---

To articulate the past historically does not mean to recognize it "the way it really was" (Ranke). It means to seize hold of a memory as it flashes up at a moment of danger.

Walter Benjamin, "On the Concept of History"

When reading theories of the public sphere, I am mostly preoccupied with the bodies in the streets, homes, industrial spaces and gardens.[1] Of less interest are the elitist debates typically presented as the core of the public in classical liberal theories of the public sphere, such as that of Jürgen Habermas. I know both theoretically but also from experience that there are embodied, resistant and critical forms of politics that require a theory of the public sphere to go beyond talking heads, a theory that embraces all of those either excluded from the dominant conceptualization of the public or marginalized while trying to take part in it. Classical theories of the public sphere, which conveniently follow Aristotelian divisions of the people into "tools" (Aristotle's word for slaves), the elitist group of *zoon politikon* and all the rest of (the largely unimportant) humans foreclose a theory and practice of the public of a genuinely common nature. In Aristotle's work—still fundamental for theories of the public sphere, be it that of Habermas or Arendt—the "rest" includes women, children, servants, the poor and those who could not produce documents for three generations of ancestors living in the city before them. It did not embrace the publics made in the streets, homes, factories, fields, forests and so on. This helps to explain why the most important political agencies involved in today's protests are relegated outside of the public sphere.

The long-term consequences of these exclusions cannot be overstated. Without systematically revising the concept and practice of the public sphere, we will not move any further forward. I am not alone in the conviction that such critical revising is crucial, and failing to do so risks shoring up the marginalization and exclusion of the political voices of the "Others" who also constitute European subjects. Denouncing the public sphere entirely makes its exclusions even stronger. Efforts to talk about something "entirely different," whether bodies or street processes, still allows for the marginalization of the political voices and claims produced there. It also perpetuates a macho, Eurocentrist model of politics. Only a strong re-appropriation of the public by those excluded will change the distribution of power and the diffusion of visibility in contemporary politics.

Even if we protest in the streets, or silently, we add to the discursive political practice, and we cannot afford to further exclude marginalized voices, including the silenced and deformed ones. As Karl Marx wrote in his *Eighteenth Brumaire of Louis Bonaparte*, representation matters, and at the same time its patterns are misleading, since the oppressed tend to vote against their class interest. As Gayatri Spivak makes clear in *Can the Subaltern Speak?*, we can run from representation but it will still be there, shaping our political agency as ineffective due to the chasm between our interests and political choices. This is where ideology comes in. If we consider Marx's and Spivak's critiques of the mechanisms of political representation seriously, we need to work on the concept of the public sphere, otherwise its mechanisms of exclusion and ideological shifts will still control our political theory and practice.

The theories of counterpublics discussed here contest the exclusions and bias inherent in Habermas's notion of the public sphere; however, they likewise evade the question of how not to repeat these problematic mechanisms. Inspired by the notion of the common as it was presented by Negri and Hardt, as well as Félix Guattari's concept of transversality, I offer some solutions. Every political option leaves its traces in the discursive field and political debates. Leaving this large field of articulated consent to the liberals is to me like abandoning the ship in the middle of a marine battle. Why would we want to do such thing? Resigning from any theoretical and practical influence on the public sphere because liberal and conservative politics shaped it to ideologically strengthen the hegemony of these leading political currents means allowing the continuation of the exclusionary political practice we have known until now. Today the possibilities of a globalized fight for equality are the greatest in history, and the spread of the women's protests since 2016 proves my point very eloquently—yet our concepts of the public, and the public sphere in particular, mainly exclude their voices, helping to perpetuate their marginalization.

In her analysis of the Occupy movement, the "we, the people" formula and public gatherings, Judith Butler rightly defends the role of nondiscursive elements in constituting a people or peoples.[2] Accentuating the performative dimensions of this constitution, she solves the classical dilemma of those in and out of the public sphere. But Butler's analysis, while far more focused on the "bodies in the streets" than Habermas's and other liberal theories of the public sphere, nevertheless shares the assumption that the making of the people builds a sense of togetherness based on a chain of words and actions that include—or at least reference—the basic "we, the people" formula. Interestingly, Butler emphasises the connection between the right of assembly and the legal guarantee of the right to strike and form labor unions, thus implicitly evoking the Solidarność movement, which was the first massive mobilization making claims based on the 1976 International Covenant on Civil and Political Rights (ICCPR), which she references in her text. This connection—between the possibility of making economic claims and the right to publicly voice demands through assembly—is deepened by a growing precarization, pushing people in so many countries to form the Occupy movement, to participate in the protests in Turkey, Egypt, Tunisia and other countries and to build the M15 movement in Spain. However, the mechanism of street protest—as important as it was in the years after the economic crisis of 2008—has failed in multiple ways, one of which is a lack of institutional structure. The rise of such political parties as Podemos in Spain, Syriza in Greece, the Peoples' Democratic Party (HDP) in Turkey or Razem in Poland was precisely a follow-up and a transition from these protests in an effort to translate their politics into more stable and possibly also more effective means of political agency.

Butler is right to summarize the events of Gezi Park, the Occupy movement and the other protests of the time as particularly vital examples of public gatherings that express the general constitution of the people as heterogeneous, embodied and contextualized against market forces. I believe that these remarks correctly diagnose the weak points of many liberal theories of the public sphere and allow for their critique and correction. Butler is also right when she claims that every act of constituting the public sphere immediately brings forth the risk of imprisonment. One might not actually be arrested or threatened or encounter violence or death—yet every act of public protest entails such risk. It only depends on the particular time and place as to whether this risk is big or small. This part of Butler's argument is an important correction to the predominantly optimistic liberal visions of the public sphere, in which becoming public is portrayed as immersing oneself in a zone of wisdom, while in fact the majority of efforts to become public are done with risk—especially those performed by those who clearly stand outside of elitist liberal vision of public sphere participants. The all-too-frequent reality of violence, imprisonment or death can be seen in the striking example of the US civil rights movement: its main leaders, Martin Luther King Jr. and Malcolm X, murdered and other key representatives imprisoned. Also, the history of the Polish opposition after 1945 is filled with instances of people being imprisoned and even killed. This dangerous element—by which I mean making certain matters and people public—is absent not only in liberal theories of the public sphere (Habermas being my favorite example), but also from leftist theories of counterpublics, such as those of Alexander Kluge and Oskar Negt as well as Nancy Fraser. Michael Warner, who wrote about Black and queer counterpublics, among others, has emphasized the cost at which public agency takes place.[3] Similarly, Butler is right to mention the risk of imprisonment, but she is wrong in not mentioning the threat of death. This reality is very real in many places around the globe, such as in Turkey where, during a police raid on a meeting of the HDP, dozens of members were killed. In some countries, going to demonstrations seems perfectly safe, yet in most places it is connected with at least some risk.

I am aware that revisiting Habermas's theory of the public sphere may strike many as mundane. Around 2013, when I started to research Solidarność and counterpublics, everybody was convinced there was little to say about Habermas's thinking in relation to these things. But I believe that certain aspects of his theory correctly capture the present reality of the public sphere; others help to shape its ideological power over the imaginations of not just conservative politicians, but also the progressive left. Also, the opposition to Habermas's thinking—particularly the theories of Kluge and Negt, with their vision of proletarian counterpublic spheres, Nancy Fraser's feminist counterpublics and Michael Warner's analysis of publics and counterpublics—are extremely helpful in a left-wing reshaping of our understanding of the public beyond liberal and conservative political thinking. For example, regarding the notion that a public and private divide is crucial for the making of politics, feminists have made of this divide one of the worst demons of patriarchy and declared its abolition, with slogans such as "the personal is political," as well as harshly criticizing the ways in which this division has perpetuated the invisibility of domestic violence, women's care and affective labor as well as reproductive work. Since the 1970s, we have not seen a major repetition of this annihilation, while the majority of institutional politics still works based on this distinction, thus maintaining the exclusions it traditionally caused. While some may say that "the work seems to have been done," the theory and practice of politics remains shaped by what enters the public and what stays private. As I will detail, in Habermas's theory of the public sphere, this division allows us to shut down the Pandora's box of particularism—the entire sector of production, and that of reproduction, are excluded from the debate as insufficiently liberated from the domain of needs. But if politics is not about needs, what is it about? When the issue of equal rights is discussed, do we discuss its theoretical forms or its actualization in the existing society? When Kluge and Negt say they want to discuss the public spheres of production, they also speak about desires, bringing in Wilhelm Reich and his analysis of the mass psychology of fascism, warning that embodiment can become a tool for the left but also a dangerous weapon of the right. Yet they discuss desire as an element of what they call, after Benjamin, "lived experience," and in this they situate production, but also the politics implied by psychological drives.[4] In today's analysis, the early days of Solidarność are usually nostalgically petrified into a pseudo-utopian mythology of the once brave nation that is long past. The sheer possibility of approaching the events of 1980 and 1981 is conveniently blocked by the supposedly definitive character of the events that took place later, especially the martial law introduced in 1981 and the neoliberal transformation that began after 1989. This idealized and stabilized vision of a securely distanced political event usually becomes an argument for the impossibility of any general political mobilization today.[5] "Solidarity's failure,"[6] the "self-limiting revolution,"[7] "Polish uprising" and other idioms petrify the beginnings of Solidarność into a "bad abstraction," a pseudo-utopia contradicting its basic principle—it does not aim at negating the status quo, but affirms and stabilizes its appearance.

This nostalgic petrification is understandable, as the memories of Solidarność are loaded with trauma. A common political agency, hope and sense of change was awakened in August 1980 and explored by most of the society, but it was painfully foreclosed on December 13, 1981, when martial law was imposed in Poland, resulting not only in the despair and resignation of the majority of Solidarność members, but also in the erased memory of the political agency of the masses, predominantly the workers and women.* The necessary transition of Solidarność into an underground movement, enforced by its de-legalization and the arrest of the 3,000 most active members on and after December 13, 1981, required the anonymity of those who decided to stay active. The mass arrest also eliminated certain spoken

---

* This is a common image of the events, available in every source that discusses these years.

forms of political agency, such as big meetings, debates and discussion, making way for written formats of expression only accessible for those already fluent in this form of political engagement—principally, those educated in political analysis and law. It therefore re-established the classic division of workers—actively conspiring as printers and distributers of the clandestine Solidarność press—and intellectuals, engaging in debates via illegal press and radio, which was obviously exclusive. The proletarian counterpublics were easily appropriated by those with more cultural capital. It was thus much easier to "forget" the worker's own circulation of knowledge and political agency, which founded Solidarność, and insert it in a line of the oppositional movements in Poland that had been initiated by the intelligentsia.

For that reason, and due to the enthusiastic welcoming of neo-liberal capitalism to Poland after 1989, Lauren Berlant's notion of "cruel optimism" is an interesting tool to unpack the unfulfilled promises of Solidarność. Berlant depicts it in the following passage:

> A relation of cruel optimism exists when something you desire is actually an obstacle to your flourishing. It might involve food, or a kind of love; it might be a fantasy of the good life, or a political project ... These kinds of optimistic relation are not inherently cruel. They become cruel only when the object that draws your attachment actively impedes the aim that brought you to it initially.[8]

This concept depicts an affective attachment, of which the object not only ceases to fulfill the premises it once was chosen to keep, but it also becomes the source of the subject's confusion and a danger to the desiring subject. Berlant goes on to explain:

> But, again, optimism is cruel when the object of scene that ignites a sense of possibility actually makes it impossible to attain the expansive transformation for which a person or a people risks striving; and, doubly, it is cruel insofar as the very pleasures of being inside a relation have become sustaining regardless of the content of the relation, such that a person or a world finds itself

bound to a situation of profound threat that is, at the same time, profoundly confirming.[9]

Solidarność was created in a highly democratic, popular, massive and yet not destructive atmosphere of resistance and opposition. It was unequivocally desired by the majority of the Polish population. By March 1981, some 10 million had officially registered as its members, and belief in the transformative power of this entity was huge. However, the economic and political reforms introduced after 1989 left the majority of the population disenchanted and resistant to the very idea of using popular mobilization to transform politics. The "defeat of Solidarity," depicted by David Ost, consisted of cruel optimism—its premises were not only unfulfilled but, in reality, it became the exact opposite of what had been decided in the Solidarność committee meetings in 1980 and 1981.[10] Today's problem, however, consists not only of the fact that the liberals cannot defeat the right wing in Poland, as Ost emphasizes. The main political problem caused by "the defeat of Solidarity" is actually profoundly structural, a systemic condition of the day-to-day practices of politics: the working classes, women and minorities cannot produce any reliable representation other than that granted to them through the populist structures of right-wing politics.

The counterpublics of Solidarność that I would like to discuss here concern only the first sixteen months of its existence (August 1980–December 1981) and I do not pretend to offer a complete account either of the events from this period or of subsequent events. Instead I interpret Solidarność as a form of proletarian counterpublic, following the idea introduced by Elżbieta Matynia of discussing Solidarność as a structural transformation of the public sphere.[11] In my discussion concerning the character of that public sphere, I discover the limitations of Habermas's theory, and argue for implementing theories of counterpublics that were written in critical response to his work. An important element of such an interpretation of Solidarność is acknowledging the workers' political agency and emphasizing their experience in the production process. The specifics of this experience and its influence on both the form and content of Solidarność's political agency requires an introduction to the concept of proletarian counterpublics, but it also allows for grasping the utopian aspect of these formidable events. If we decide to see utopia as the background and direct precursor of the more scientifically inclined project of Marxism, as Bronisław Baczko does in his collected essays on utopia in *Wyobrażenia społeczne* (*The Social Imaginaries*), then the political mobilization, resistance and victory of the working masses definitely constitutes a disclosure of the left.[12] As important as utopia is to understanding the multilayered character of the transformation brought on by Solidarność, within the first two years of its existence, I believe, its circumstances required a more contemporary theoretical framework than the notion provided in the classic sixteenth- and nineteenth-century versions. I would therefore like to introduce the concept of counterpublics, of which certain aspects clearly allow for emphasizing the utopian aspects of Solidarność. In an effort to include experience, trauma and affect in this analysis, too, I follow Kluge and Negt in their effort to build a plebeian alternative to the bourgeois public sphere as it was depicted by Habermas.[13]

There is something interesting in examining the utopian dimensions of Solidarność, and there are very good reasons for undertaking such a task. It was largely inspired by the work of Edward Abramowski, the most prominent Polish theorist of anarcho-communism and one of the leading inventors of the cooperative movement in Poland and globally. Abramowski's texts were fundamental for some Solidarność leaders, including Andrzej Gwiazda, Joanna Duda-Gwiazda, as well as for Jacek Kuroń and Karol Modzelewski—the two notorious Marxist critics of state communism. Modzelewski is actually said to have proposed the name of Solidarność to the union. The utopian dimension of Solidarność also lies in its origin—the general strike had been an anarchist utopia for several decades. The idea of a pacifist transition also sounds positively utopian, and although Gandhi and his movement in India tend to be seen as a realization of such impossibility, there remains quite a lot of the impossible in pacifism practiced on a large scale. Utopia can be seen as a distant relative of critical theory's "regulative ideal," embraced by the concept of counterpublics, albeit only tacitly. It may also be located in the disagreement and anti-institutionalism of theories of the common, demanding new forms (of institutions, of constituent power, of struggle) that should be read as utopian, although Hardt and Negri would probably dislike the risk of transcendentalism in it.

In their conversation on utopia, published in *The Utopian Function of Art and Literature,* Theodor Adorno and Ernst Bloch agreed that utopian thinking requires a rejection of the necessity of death.[14] Only a vision of a life worth living eternally, a life of which the eternity does not seem dreadful or scary, constitutes a solid base for utopia. Adorno says it very explicitly: "I believe that without the notion of an unfettered life, freed from death, the idea of *the* utopia cannot even be thought at all."[15] Because of this intrinsic connection with death—or, actually, because of the necessary negation of death in any utopia—it requires a negative stance toward determinism, finitude and the status quo. I believe that this stance was taken by the workers of the Gdańsk Shipyard when they began to strike on August 14, 1980, which led to the regional strike and massive solidarity strikes across Poland, involving some 700 workplaces (and the majority of the important ones) and some 700,000 workers—which today we tend to see as a general strike.[16] The strike began in solidarity with elderly crane operator Anna Walentynowicz, once a heroine of the working class, who later critiqued and joined the resistance to the state apparatus. After the rise in prices of alimentary products in the summer of 1980, she told her boss that life under such conditions is not worth surviving; this recalls the great revival of utopia, namely the 1960s, when Debord, Vaneigem and other situationists would say almost the same—that under capitalism life became about surviving. The workers rebuffed the legitimate fear of state violence; they were also cautious that any negotiations with only the local authorities would lead nowhere, as had been the case in numerous strikes and negotiations in 1970 and 1971. Around this time, the shipyards of Szczecin tried to compromise with the local Communist Party leaders, without result. The stories of some sixty workplaces from northern Poland, including Gdańsk, Gdynia, Elbląg, Kwidzyn, Malbork, Szczecin, Gryfino and Stargard, have been carefully recounted by Roman Laba in *The Roots of Solidarity.*[17] So, in 1980, the strikers of the Gdańsk shipyard demanded that the central committee of the Communist Party of Poland negotiate with them. This was also inspired by the textile workers of Łódź, who demanded the same in 1971 and were the only protest after WWII that was successful until 1980. It also must be stressed that the majority of workers of the textile industry in Łódź were women.

Bronisław Baczko interrogates the meaning of utopia for Thomas More and responds with a twofold query: How should this key word be understood? Does it mean *Ou*-topia, a land that "is nowhere," one that does not exist? Or is it a *Eu*-topia, the best of lands, even better than that recalled by Plato? Or perhaps we find here two meanings, simultaneously: the best political community possible to imagine, which is proven by the text, yet exists nowhere except in the imagination and knowledge shaping this imagination?[18] Baczko further emphasized that those creating utopias "disenchant heavens and their mythical time and space. However, by the same token, they also create competing or even alternative imaginaries." Differently put, negation of the status quo is utopia's fundamental function.[19]

In the case of the world desired by Solidarność, one that had a chance to be transversally put into practice after the 1980 August Agreements between the strikers and the Polish authorities' representatives, both aspects—the non-existence (until then) and the goodness (compared to the inegalitarian, selective and exploitative reality of the state)—have been vividly present since the beginning. Their demands were diverse: an independent workers' union; the end of censorship; freedom of the press and media; the release of political prisoners. These things seemed just as important as work-free Saturdays, lowering the age of retirement and lengthening maternity leave, ensuring there were sufficient places in daycare facilities. Together these demands covered various parts of social life and were to activate the transformation of society in its different aspects.[20] But Solidarność cannot be reduced to the twenty-one demands of the striking workers. The movement was catalyzed by possibility—a sudden urge to actually engage in the country's politics, changing them and being involved in this process. Most accounts of this time, including that offered by Elżbieta Matynia, support my claim that it was the moment in Polish history when the greatest proportion of society was actively engaged in changing the country.

If compared to earlier versions of the workers' postulates from December 1970 and early 1971, such as the twenty-one demands from the Szczecin shipyard or the thirty-five postulates of the workers of the Port of Gdańsk, the twenty-one demands from August 1980 were less critical and more positive, thus expressing a move toward another future. For example, in 1970 and 1971, at least one demand pertained to "cuts in bureaucracy"; Elbląg workers elaborated it most straightforwardly as "cutting bureaucracy by two-thirds" or "we demand comrade Kociołek's apology to the working class for calling them hooligans, etc."[21]

Due to its spatiotemporality, Solidarność might seem more fitting in the Foucauldian theory of heterotopia.[22] When we understand Solidarność as the result of existing, often contradictory conditions, situated in historical time and sharing the ambivalences of its conditions, the union could be seen as a good example of the heterogeneous entity depicted by Foucault. As he observes: "There are also, probably in every culture, in every civilization, real places—places that do exist and that are formed in the very founding of society—which are something like counter-sites, a kind of effectively enacted utopia in which the real sites, all the other real sites that can be found within the culture, are simultaneously represented, contested, and inverted." Solidarność was granted a presence through existing laws, and it demanded equality and respect for the workers—as did communist Poland's political doctrine at the time (sadly, not anymore).

Solidarność did not contest the most general aspects of socialist reality, though. The twenty-one demands were not directed to overthrow communism; one could even claim that they were formulated in order to fulfill the socialist premises of the Polish state. Solidarność did not explicitly mention revolutionary political change. However, as Zbigniew Kowalewski rightly emphasizes in his account of the events, had the demands been put in practice, the system would have imploded.[23] Solidarność is therefore best described as a realized utopia, a sudden intrusion of a different reality but which did not fully dismantle the older one. The key elements discussed here—the union's demands, democratic forms of organization and numbers of people involved—seem somewhat utopian, especially today. Yet between 1980 and 1981, they were actual aspects—matters of fact—of Poland's social reality.

It should perhaps be emphasized that in his 1967 lecture, Foucault used the term "counter-sites," which I find particularly significant, as it almost sounds like "counterpublics." By using counter-sites to discuss heterotopias, he meant that by their very existence, the latter contest and object to the existing reality. This is what Solidarność did to Poland's state apparatus in 1980, including the Communist Party. Uniting all social strata, but with workers at its core, it unmasked the privilege-based structures of the party, modeling what workers' organization should actually look like, without openly criticizing the party.

Counterpublics in fact involve more than just undermining the principles of the entity being opposed—they require the political involvement and discursive agency of those participating; they also involve the transformation of structures of representation. *Pace* the Foucauldian notion of heterotopia, I would like to suggest that in the case of Solidarność, we approach more critical and engaged events, thus exceeding the supposedly disengaged character of heterotopia. What I am proposing also differs from Foucault's examples in other ways. I am thinking in particular about his reference to medieval convents, which operated on the margins of societies. By contrast, Solidarność installed itself at the core of Poland's state-communist society, in factories and other workplaces. And instead of cultivating alternative lifestyles, the union actually transformed society on every level—in a word, transversally, as I have discussed.*

---

* Here I enter a friendly polemic with a colleague, Cezary Rudnicki, who discusses Solidarność as an example of what Foucault called *parrhesia*. His article is a great addition to Solidarność studies; however, I disagree in fundamental ways to reading the whole of Solidarność as a form of "telling the truth"; I believe it is very reductive and repeats the exclusion of the working class's political agency to merely "ethics." Solidarność built laws, institutions, decision-making procedures, culture and even poetry, it governed workplaces and other institutions, and it contributed to the transition of the political

In Polish history, intellectual elites and the working classes rarely cooperated. Many historians have emphasized this lack of alignment, including those working on Solidarność, such as Andrzej Friszke. The events of 1980 had the utopian resonance, both *ou*-topian and *eu*-topian. The workers of different classes, in the "supposedly class-less society," as Sławomir Magala brilliantly called it, including workers of what was called the "working intelligentsia" labored together in solidarity to transform Polish politics, society and culture.[24] In other words, the main division in Polish society—the key reason for the failures of the previous efforts to transform the society in 1956, 1968 and 1970—was temporarily sublated in the process of cooperation.

I have carefully chosen my language and used the words "politics," "society" and "culture" because these were the registers on which the transformation introduced by Solidarność actually operated. In order to understand what this entailed, we must look beyond the general label of the supposed "apoliticality" of Solidarność assigned to it by many different authors, for different reasons. For instance, Jadwiga Staniszkis, author of the famous analysis of the events of 1980–1 entitled *Poland's Self-Limiting Revolution,* first published in 1983 in English, suggests that due to its mainly ethical focus, Solidarność was not political enough.[25] In this and the majority of other accounts, the notion of politics seems very much inscribed in institutions—and it is thus also quite ancient. Interestingly, the discussion between lawyers concerning the topic of whether Solidarność was a revolution or not still seems open, as it definitely changed the doctrine of the state (into a workers' democracy, based on councils), but the process of this change was so particular, unusual and short term that it is very hard to measure its status.[26]

It was clear that the straightforward demand to change the most general definition of the political system would lead to military

---

system in Poland, as well as to its legal order. It therefore requires a wider conceptual framework that can embrace this heterogeneity of practices, and thus I believe the notion of counterpublics is better suited to express Solidarność's actions. See C. Rudnicki, "Jeśli mówić prawdę, to tylko w Sierpniu. Etyka jako polityka," *Praktyka Teoretyczna* 4: 22, 2016.

intervention from the allied forces of the Soviet Bloc, as had happened in Hungary in 1956 and in Czechoslovakia in 1968. But does resignation from a revolutionary shift of the system immediately signify that the character of Solidarność was apolitical? I believe that Solidarność actually *requires* such a vision of politics, in which warm soup for the port workers in winter (an actual demand of the workers of the Port of Gdańsk in 1970) constitutes a political matter, as does the age of retirement, the end of censorship and the creation of independent workers' unions. I also think that the majority of contemporary theories of power, including those based around concepts of hegemony, ideology or biopolitics, allow an understanding of Solidarność as political par excellence. Theories of the public sphere likewise offer this opportunity—and thus the argument of Elżbieta Matynia was so important—although their limitations regarding the bourgeois classes demand further investigation, which is possible through theories of proletarian and feminist counterpublics.

The concept of the public sphere as it is framed in Habermas's seminal analysis excludes the workers' public sphere as "historically insignificant."[27] Not only does this theory limit itself to bourgeois public spheres, it also strengthens the already formidable exclusion of workers' political agency, rendering the public spheres of women, immigrants and the precariat virtually nonexistent. This serial exclusion has been critiqued by various historians, such as Geoff Eley and Mary Ryan; philosophers, including Nancy Fraser[28] and Warren Montag;[29] and cultural theorists such as Michael Warner.[30] The first major critique, however, was formulated in *Public Sphere and Experience* by Alexander Kluge and Oskar Negt, who focus here on the (factory) workers' public sphere, delivering the most systematic analysis of counterpublics. In their view, counterpublics are oppositional in two ways: they resist not only the state apparatus and its ideology but also the cultural elites, whose hegemonic position makes the public sphere always already exclusionary to those of the working classes.[31] Habermas's public sphere can only be singular, because plural spheres would corrupt his theory's general character. Moreover, his public sphere is based on a strict distinction between the public and the private, by which the latter cannot enter politics as a representation of particular issues. This formula repeats the classical Greek demand of politics as formulated by Aristotle and other thinkers.[32] In later times, the exclusion of *oikos,* home matters, also included the exclusion of the *oikonomia,* the laws of the home, later translated as "economy." It is fascinating how strongly this exclusion marks not only the idea of the public sphere for Habermas, but also the dominant reading of Solidarność as "apolitical." In Kluge and Negt's formulation of counterpublics, production occupies the central position in two senses: as a social process of value production mediated by capital as well as the production of subjectivity. The same mechanisms of commodification appear when a commodity and an experience are produced—with a distinction, however: within the bourgeois public sphere, those who express the cause of the workers immediately become the traitors of that cause.[33] The dialectics of the subject formation within the symbolic codes of production are always generating its subaltern—the workers—who cannot speak within the existing public sphere.

In "The Lost Treasure of Solidarity," Matynia rightly claims that the "carnival of Solidarność," as the sixteen months of it were commonly called, consisted of a communicative utopia, where the artificial talk of party elites was replaced with a meaningful language created in demands, debates and negotiation that involved the majority of the Polish population. This utopia of a common language brings to mind an image from Walter Benjamin's "The Task of the Translator," notably the pure language that "[emerges] as from the harmony of all the various ways of meaning."[34] Matynia summarizes the results of the August Agreements (the agreement between Solidarność and the government, signed August 31, 1980 with all twenty-one demands accepted) as "an astonishingly speedy shift from the private to the public," signaled by the institutional formula of the independent, self-governing workers' unions and the ability "to say whatever we want."[35]

I believe there was an emergence of a series of very different counterpublics—those of workers, women, intelligentsia, party members, all engaged in a process of creating a heterogeneous, multilayered public sphere, replacing the homogeneous, elitist one. There are several reasons why this cannot be limited to or even perceived as the classical, bourgeois public sphere of Habermas. First, there was no classical bourgeoisie in state-communist Poland. Second, even if the intelligentsia and the ruling party officials were structurally similar to the Western bourgeoisie, they were not the only participants in the August Agreements; the opposition was composed of 700,000 striking workers of diverse social strata and only a small percentage of them had a higher education. And third, discussing the counterpublics of Solidarność rather than a Habermasian understanding of the public sphere seems more intuitive, because a plethora of conflicted interests was expressed in the demands and negotiations in August 1980. Some of them were "political" in the traditional sense, for example, the demand to end censorship. But others, such as rehiring Anna Walentynowicz, providing a sufficient amount of childcare (yes! Just like in socialist feminism) or lowering the retirement age were demands that would probably not be seen as fully political by Habermas and most of the liberal thinkers of the time, and perhaps also not today. Some of the demands simply cut across the public and private distinction, which makes them a part of counterpublics rather than the classical public sphere.

To say that the demand for a better system of childcare becomes public is a simplification. Yet as a political demand, it connotes gender issues and therefore undermines the public/private distinction, as Carole Pateman and other feminist philosophers would surely claim.[36] What may seem utopian in the August Agreements of 1980 and later is actually the sudden dismantlement of the strict public/private divide. More specifically, what was utopian about this process was the explosion of debate and other forms of public exchange. Suddenly the issues—soup for the freezing workers of the Port of Gdańsk, the age of retirement or the end of censorship—were freely debated by everyone in any form, and soon after the signing of the agreements in 1980, some of those diverse issues actually became topics of the negotiations concerning various changes in Polish law.

Some basic facts concerning Solidarność should be listed here. The strike in the Gdańsk shipyard, in solidarity with Anna Walentynowicz, begun on August 14, 1980, and solidarity strikes at other workplaces in Poland started immediately, as soon as workers were called upon by those at the shipyard and others. In order to imagine the importance of this strike, we must think of one of the key industrial sites in Poland, hiring some 30,000 workers, of which one-third were women. The shipyard covered the territory of a small town, had its own buses, bars and cultural center. It produced ships, so it was also a port, with dozens of big and small metal workshops and high cranes, capable of carrying several tonnes of metal each. Men and women were doing the physical work, and some of the women were also in the offices. Women were said to be the best crane operators, it was assumed they were more responsible, which was lifesaving, as parts of the ship were often carried by cranes over the heads of other workers. Some smaller workplaces decided to join the strike immediately, including the city bus and tramways network. Henryka Krzywonos, the tramway driver central to the prolongation of the strike after Walentynowicz was promised to be rehired and the only woman to sign the agreements on August 31, 1980, is famous for stopping her tram in the center of Gdańsk, right next to the opera, and declaring, "This tramway ain't going any further," thus blocking traffic at a strategic junction and informing the city inhabitants that the shipyard was on strike. This was vital, because other communication, such as the telephone lines, had been cut across Gdańsk immediately after the strike began.[37] The strikers quickly decided on the twenty-one demands and the strike spread throughout the majority of the country. The government was called to discuss the twenty-one demands at the Gdańsk shipyard and its delegates arrived on August 25. Finally, on August 31, 1980, an agreement was signed, leading to the legalization of the independent workers' unions, a salary increase, the release of political prisoners and a general agreement for the democratization of workplaces. This led to the "carnival of Solidarność," which, in fact, involved thousands of Polish men and women as they deliberatively transformed workplaces and institutions across the country.

To understand the scale of this change, we need to consider some numbers. After the registration of Solidarność in autumn 1980, by March of 1981 approximately 10 million were official members of the union, out of Poland's entire population of 36 million at the time. In 1980, the Polish Communist Party counted some 3 million members and the Soviet Communist Party some 11 million members. When we look at these numbers, it is easy to think that Solidarność constituted a sort of "accomplished utopia." Through the union's mass mobilization, almost one-third of the Polish population was involved.[38] Today, such scale helps to imagine a genuinely popular movement. It also sounds positively scary, as most of us probably do not have experience of being part of such a mobilization.

Briefly, we could say that Solidarność was galvanized by the agency of workers, who eventually invited delegates of the "intelligentsia" to become their advisors but who, however, began and organized the movement on their own. This means that the multilayered negotiations between workplaces, and later between the protesting workers and the government, were run predominantly by members of the working class. However, this would seem implausible in Habermas's analysis of the public sphere. In the preface to his book *The Structural Transformation of the Public Sphere*, Habermas openly claims that "it [the public sphere] refers to those features of a historical constellation that attained dominance and leaves aside the plebeian public sphere as a variant that in a sense was suppressed in the historical process."[39] It is rather clear that the very appearance and later significance of Solidarność undermines the presumption of the supposedly irrelevant character of the plebeian publics. But as Geoff Eley and others have demonstrated, the historical presence and influence of subaltern groups, such as the nineteenth-century peasants or other workers, is not difficult to document. Therefore, it should be noted that, as Eley eloquently demonstrates:

> The liberal disideratum of reasoned exchange also became available for nonbourgeois, subaltern groups, whether the radical intelligentsia of Jacobinism and its successors or wide sections of social classes like the peasantry or the working class . . . That is, the positive values of the liberal public sphere quickly acquired broader democratic resonance, with the resulting emergence of impressive popular movements.[40]

The rise of Solidarność was by far the biggest transformation of the public sphere in decades, in Poland and beyond. As such, it broke all the basic principles of classical understandings of the "public sphere" as the domain of educated, privileged men. Women were visible and present at the beginning of Solidarność, as was the working class; these people literally ran the protests, strikes and negotiations. Therefore, perhaps it is through the "experience of the working class" that we should account for these events? Kluge and Negt demand a reflexive notion of experience, one situated in a historical context; as they argue, the public sphere operates according to the rule of private use, not according to the rules whereby the experiences and class interests of workers are organized. The interests of workers appear in the bourgeois public sphere as nothing more than a gigantic, cumulative "private interest," not as the collective mode of production for quantitatively new forms of public sphere and public interest.

Kluge and Negt immediately unmask the mechanism of the always already failed representation of such working-class interest in the public sphere: it is always already a misrepresentation.[41] Solidarność, with its ability to use the general strike, appealed to the universality of the workers' claims, which according to liberal political thinking are always reduced to particularity, as economic issues rooted in basic needs and therefore belonging to the private sphere. The general solidarity strike with the Gdańsk shipyard, which spread around Poland within days, combined with the democratic management of the strike's committees, and later different branches of the legalized Solidarność were orchestrated mainly by the workers themselves, including women. Kluge and Negt's "dialectic concept of experience" allows them to address the realities of workers, shaped by factories, the extraction of capital, and the experiences of alienation and commodification. Yet these insights do not lead them to embrace the experience of women, which was invisible in their work when they began in 1972 and was only welcomed to their social analysis in their later book, *History and Obstinacy,* published in 2008 (and in English only in an abbreviated version in 2014).[42]

Kluge and Negt open their *Public Sphere and Experience* by declaring that their aim is to discuss the "use-value of the public sphere" and to investigate how and to what extent the working class can use this realm for their ends.[43] They immediately discover that the

"experience" in which the bourgeois public sphere is rooted is one
belonging to the upper classes. As a result, the workers' experience is
not only excluded from it, but this exclusion is perpetuated even in
situations where workers could try to use the existing public sphere as
a tool for their interest. In *Public Sphere and Experience,* the authors
claim that the liberal public sphere confronts the workers with the
totality of the bourgeois experience as ideology. Kluge and Negt challenged this exclusive vision of the public sphere and, in turn, proposed
an alternative, one that allows us to see the public sphere not as a
matter of "a handful of specialists" but as a social entity, constituted
by society as a whole, in particular conditions of production. They
therefore articulate class conflict following Marx and install it at the
core of their definition of the public sphere, which led to the idea of
counterpublics: a counter public sphere of workers who are opposed
to the capitalist powers both in state power and in its privileged opposition. Proletarian counterpublics account for the experience of
production, and they move beyond the Aristotelian division of public/
private that constitutes Habermas's public sphere. The experience
that could lead to solidarity is depicted as a sense of togetherness in
production but also in the process of establishing a common revolt.
As in the analysis of fascism by Wilhelm Reich, Kluge and Negt also
emphasize the risk of this solidarity being appropriated by fascist
forces. They add a critique of the commercial media to this issue, in
which they follow Habermas, whose "fear of the media" they share, as
Fredric Jameson and Dana Polan rightly observe.[44] Jameson shows
how a passive, unidirectional interpretation of media agency blurs the
opportunity for response, transformation and even *détournement* of
media messages by their users or participants. As Jameson and Polan
emphasize, since the cultural theory of media of the 1960s and 1970s,
it is impossible to maintain this passive interpretation of audiences
and publics more generally. A larger discussion of the role of media
for social movements, politics and the counterpublics of the common
appears in this book in Chapter 3.

As a counterpublic, Solidarność was heterogeneous. It spilled over
the agenda of the classical, bourgeois public sphere because the union
undermined any public/private division. Differently from Matynia,

though, I do not see the demands of the striking workers in Gdańsk in 1980 as compatible with what Habermas calls "general" and "universal"; on the contrary, they were—as Kluge and Negt rightly argue—always already doomed to particularity, and the "private" sphere, which does not disclose their "generality," only requires the overcoming of the public/private divide. However, what is worse is that some of their claims could very well have been part of the bourgeois public sphere. I am thinking in particular about their demand to stop the state censorship of publications. In this hybridity of claims lies, I think, the biggest weakness of any spontaneous demands from a political entity that is not in the classical, bourgeois public sphere, from the perspective of the liberal public. In the perspective I am developing following Kluge and Negt, however, this is their biggest strength, as they constitute a transversal transformation rather than an external critique. Such political demands are situated, embodied and contextualized; they do not appear as a "bad abstract" and thus can bring political change much more easily than demands built in one class or group within the society and imposed as representative of society as a whole.

In Guattari's *The Three Ecologies*, we find a notion of change that depicts the kind that Solidarność brought to Polish politics.[45] It was neither merely a protest nor a reform nor an alternative. Solidarność moved between clusters and levels of society, culture, politics and forms of organization, combining ordinary matters with exceptional claims; bridging new and old formats of debate; blurring private and public matters. In *The Three Ecologies*, which in many ways develops certain elements of *A Thousand Plateaus,* Guattari argues for political analysis without separation. This is an analysis in which the molecular and global are understood as intertwined and necessary for grasping all aspects of a subject's formation. Solidarność may not have explicitly brought forward the ecological narrative, but it urged the combination rather than separation of the multiple aspects of material existence in the making of social transformation. It was definitely a movement for the common, as has been argued in very different contexts by Matynia and by Jan Sowa.[46] However, this is not an abstracted "common good," separated from the experience of

production, alienated by the philosophical formulas of empty abstrac-
ions and the ruling party's artificial speech.[47] A good example of this
artificiality is the slogan that used to be printed right below the title
of the main daily newspaper, *Trybuna Ludu* (*People's Tribune*),
"Proletarians of the world, unite!" One of my professors used to joke
that the party apparatchiks were waking up every day, buying the
newspaper in a kiosk next door, sitting down with their morning
coffee and laughing, "Unite? My ass!" And how great must have been
the party apparatchiks' surprise in August 1980, when the proletarians actually united?

The expansive presence of communist slogans, so popular in
communist Poland, might perhaps have had some influence on the
self-understanding and sense of dignity of the workers. This would
require some further study; however, it is perhaps worth noticing how
in the speeches of the shipyard workers and other people involved in
the 1980 strikes, the sense of having the leading position in society
was explicit. To date, such a study has not been done, probably because
it would prove the empowering effects of communist state propaganda on the workers and other opposition members. This propaganda
only contained distant remnants of *The Communist Manifesto*;
however, it contained constant repetitions of how workers govern the
state. And in 1980, the workers decided to make it much more real
than it ever had been. Such a study would certainly have implications
for how we regard the facts of history—namely that by 1970, workers
were already writing up their demands and presenting them to
authorities, regardless of threats and possible risks and, more importantly, without the support of the Warsaw-based intelligentsia. Such
an analysis would help us to grasp the multiplicity of actual inspirations and origins of Solidarność, which in its early days was far more
inspired by the socialist, communist and syndicalist traditions than
by the Catholic Church (which was actually hesitant about this movement and suggested ending it in August 1980). Many of us were lured
by Andrzej Wajda's movie *Man of Iron*, awarded in Cannes in 1981,
which featured the events of the summer of 1980. In that film, the
sound we constantly hear in the background is that of the Catholic
Holy Mass or church bells. It is important to stress that masses were

happening and some priests were involved; however, the strike's bulletin devoted much more attention to poems and songs written and composed by the strikers, the "strike folklore" recitals, which happened every evening during the two weeks of the strike, or political discussions (which might have started with a "God bless" greeting, particularly if Wałęsa was speaking) and not to building a Catholic Poland, but a genuinely socialist state. Only one of the twenty-one demands was about Catholicism, and it simply demanded the realization of the law, which offered each religion, not just the most popular one, some time on public media.

As I have suggested, the notion of the common might open an interesting way of theorizing Solidarność. In Hardt and Negri's *Commonwealth,* they argue the following:

> In the context of biopolitical production, by working on the common and producing the common, the multitude constantly transforms itself. This brings to mind Marx's admiration for Charles Fourier's utopian insight that the proletariat is a subject in transition, transformed through labor but also and moreover through social, cooperative, inventive activity in the time left free from the constraints of work.[48]

Hardt and Negri further write: "The self-transformation of the multitude in production, grounded in the expansion of the common, gives an initial indication of the direction of the self-rule of the multitude in the political realm."[49] This means that the utopian prospects of "what is to be done" are already included in the process of transformation, of realizing life as it should be lived, a utopia.

In Negri and Hardt's project, the multitude may become the common. The heterogeneous, affective social can build structures and political movements, which involve the environment, culture and animals—all those things that have unjustly been called "resources," including air, water and land, count as elements of the common, as well as languages, technologies and knowledges. The common is a third option, apart from private property and the public when understood as state-owned. In my reading, the commons is the sublation of this division, including non-human actors, such as the environment, animals and culture. If we look closer at definitions of the public in a European context, we will see that what Negri and Hardt argue about the common suits the key expectations often articulated about the public.[50] In classical legal texts in both Poland and Germany, public space and public institutions are constituted by society, with the support and guidance of state power. Art institutions, universities and even local parliaments are sometimes those preserving democracy, autonomy and collective decision-making. Under neoliberalism, supposedly state-run public property constitutes not only an alternative, but sometimes even a block to massive privatization. In a post-communist country such as Poland, the possibilities of restructuring public institutions into institutions of the common are not only logical, but might seem necessary. The common is even closer to counterpublics, as it is embedded in "dialectically understood" experience, as emphasized by Kluge and Negt. The counterpublics, materialized, autonomous and moving beyond the public/private divide, seem to capture the commonality and the ordinary embedded in the concept of the common just as much as they stand for solidarity in struggle. I return to the prospects of counter publics of the common in Chapter 3.

Many scholars have discussed the failure of Solidarność to accomplish its promises of solidarity. I would instead like to mention some of the important work emphasizing the proletarian character of this movement. First, there is Roman Laba's brilliant elucidation of how workers are always granted a spectrum of invisibility and exclusion in the research conducted by academics. In *The Roots of Solidarity*, he draws a rich and revealing picture of how workers are typically represented by intellectuals, with all the classist prejudice and stereotypes.[51] Laba discusses scholarly projections that are often made on workers, such as their supposed "utopianism" and "lack of democracy." He also revisits the assumption of "trickle-down" political economics of engagement and proves that the legendary influence of the intellectuals on the workers is simply not historically accurate. In my own research on Solidarność, I have discussed books by prominent Polish historians of the post-WWII political opposition in Poland, and the results were somewhat scary. Andrzej Friszke, in his main analysis of the Polish opposition in the years 1945–80, discusses the year 1970 from the perspective of Jerzy Giedroyć, a very important Paris-based Polish intellectual and publisher of the magazine *Kultura*. Friszke also draws on the impressions of Adam Michnik, a prominent oppositional intellectual from Warsaw. There is also a chapter on the Committee of the Defense of the Workers (KOR), but nothing on the political agency of the workers themselves. The book contains a chapter titled "Workers," where I expected to find some information about the thousands of striking workers in the winter of 1970–71, but there was none. Friszke only depicted, in thirty-six pages, how the KOR helped the workers. While this was very important support and it should constitute a part of the analysis of the post-WWII Polish opposition, what I missed in his account was the wave of factory strikes in North Poland and Łódź in the years 1970 and 1971, from early December till late February. That winter was particularly important for forming the workers' movement, strategizing the sit-down strike and collectively writing the demands. Some 150 workplaces went on strike, and in Szczecin it was so general that Communist Party members began calling that city "the independent republic of Szczecin." These strikes, however, were depicted by few authors, although notably by Zbigniew Kowalewski and Roman Laba. This was also the first time that the workers—mainly women!—of the textile industry in Łódź, the city of major strikes and revolution in 1905, demanded a meeting with central Communist Party representatives, bypassing the local authorities. And the government delegation, including the then-prime minister, Jaroszewicz, came to Łódź and sat down to negotiate with the textile workers in the freezing days of February 1971. After this conversation, food prices returned to pre-December 1970 levels, which was the main demand of all of the strikes. The textile workers' approach later served as an indispensable model for Solidarność when conducting its own negotiations with the government.

As I argue in the book *Kontrpubliczności ludowe i feministyczne* (*Feminist and Plebeian Counterpublics*), there was an internal channel (or were even multiple channels) for transmitting knowledge and skills between workers, without the mediation of intelligentsia, that were crucial for political action. Contrary to Andrzej Friszke and the majority of Polish historians of Solidarność, I claim that this movement and the workers' opposition to the authoritarian tactics and dimensions of the communist Polish governments between 1948 and 1990 were to a large extent inspired and fueled not merely by the intelligentsia and their symbolic capital, but also by the workers' own strategies, obstinacy, resistance, disagreement and solidarity. This included creating and transmitting knowledge and skills, constituting the specifics of the workers' political agency which is more often than not neglected or marginalized in accounts of contemporary Polish history.[52] Here I follow James Scott and his ability to see effective political agency in groups never even suspected of having any, such as the East-Asian peasants or the workers in my analysis of Solidarność. Zbyszek Kowalewski's claim that Solidarność was a workers' movement, and Roman Laba's meticulous reconstruction of the events of Szczecin in 1970 also support my perspective. I obviously agree, too, with Negri and Hardt that Solidarność was one of the "institutions of the common."[53]

Jacques Rancière's work in such books as *Proletarian Nights* or *Staging the People,* which discuss the autonomy of worker's production and transmission of knowledge independently of the upper classes and sometimes undermining them, was crucial for my own argument. It is necessary to correct historical inaccuracies and to build a more general claim about the insufficiency of the classist paradigm of intellectuals only willing to see and describe the agency of their own class, not that of others.[54]

There is an obvious risk in such corrections, depicted in the work of Spivak's critical account of the controversies with "progressive Western intellectuals" and "UN feminism." Both groups claim that they have direct access to the desires of the oppressed and act like they are capable of articulating these desires without any ideological abuses. This possibility is challenged by Spivak's argument, based in Althusser's theory of ideology, that this practice should be understood not merely as a set of (false) ideas, as it was presented by Mannheim or Arendt, but as a social exercise always masking the

structures of domination. Thus, according to Spivak, the simple question to the oppressed might not bring up an unbiased answer, free of
ideological masquerade. Likewise, declarations of "UN feminists"
that they "understand Third World women," might miss the point.[55] I
believe that Spivak's critical warnings should not be taken as a refuta-
tion of any resistance to capitalism.[56] Her aim, as she explains in
numerous interviews and lectures, is not to repeat the mistakes of the
hegemonic classes. This refusal to perpetuate the exclusions caused
by "good-willed" feminists or intellectuals is, I think, crucial not just
for robust scholarship but also for a politics that can steer us away
from a fascist future.

In *Privatizing Poland*, Elizabeth Cullen Dunn depicts the infantilization of the recent freedom fighters, who were perfectly adult in
1980 when launching Solidarność but only a decade later have to
"learn" management and democracy.[57] Dunn worked in a food factory
in southern Poland (Rzeszów) to observe and describe the transition
from a state-communist factory to a capitalist enterprise. In the years
following 1989, the workers of the Gerber-Alima food factory, mainly
women, were introduced to neoliberalism in its most shock-based
version. Their autonomy and dignity were in many ways questioned
by the measures of control and biopolitics introduced as part of the
neoliberal package.

Dunn's narrative outlines the various models of control, sometimes working similarly to the colonial infantilization of Europe's
"Other" while focusing on Polish society. Big business knew no
limits in the humiliation and degradation of Polish workers, and
only recently have voices critical of neoliberal capitalism been heard.
Some claim that the current Polish government's fascist political
tendencies are rooted in this period of humiliation and degradation
between 1989 and the introduction of the neoliberal "shock doctrine"
and EU enlargement in 2004, and I agree with this analysis. As in the
1920s and 1930s in Germany, where the sense of humiliation, degradation and poverty was at its peak, it was rather easy to direct these
sentiments toward a grandiose dream of the "Third Reich"; in 2004
in Poland, the sentiment was similar: we have fought so bravely
against the totalitarian oppression in the 1980s and earlier, where are

our winnings? This is the usual ground on which fascism is eager to grow.

Before I turn to contemporary feminist counterpublics, I would like to offer a brief account of women's participation in Solidarność. In what follows, I critically address the feminist analysis of Solidarność as male dominated, patriarchal and exclusionary toward women. Some feminist authors argue that women were invisible and marginalized in Solidarność; I believe this is only partly true. As it has been well explained by such great researchers as Shana Penn, Ewa Kondratowicz and Marta Dzido, women were not particularly welcomed as leaders, both at the beginning of Solidarność and later, after 1989.[58] In 1991, the Women's Commission of Solidarność was closed and the union adopted a conservative political line, which it occupies today when it criticizes the women's movement, feminism and demonstrations for abortion rights.

Women were engaged from the beginning of Solidarność, and some of them actually started the strike in the Gdańsk shipyard together with men—recall crane operator Anna Walentynowicz, whose firing on August 14, 1980, triggered the strike. Or tram driver Henryka Krzywonos, or nurse and political activist Alina Pienkowska. Together, these three women forced the continuation of the strike on August 16, 1980, when Lech Wałęsa and other men had their moment of doubt. These women became famous nationwide, and rightly so.

In *Solidarity's Secret,* Shana Penn focuses on the women who published *Tygodnik Mazowsze* (*Masovia Weekly*), the key periodical of the Solidarność underground, after the introduction of martial law by General Jaruzelski on December 13, 1981. Another example of scholarship that celebrates the forgotten women of Solidarność is that of Ewa Kondratowicz, who has published a series of interviews with women of the opposition in a study titled *Lipstick on the Banner.*[59] It is worth remembering that in 1980, women constituted some 30 percent of workers at the Gdańsk shipyard. They usually operated the gantry cranes, mainly inside the shipyard's buildings. Most of these women workers led a traditional family life, doing the majority of the housework. This helps to explain why many who joined the newly created Solidarność union lamented that they did not have as much time to engage as their male colleagues did. The women "had children" (apparently men do not have children, at least in Poland) and they had housework to do.*

In 1980, women's participation in Solidarność was far from invisible. Women were present in the beginning of the strikes in the Gdańsk shipyard, and they struck in Szczecin and Łódź. They also "took over" several important activities in Solidarność after its de-legalization in December 1981, mainly printing and distributing the underground press, organizing meetings and education initiatives, supporting the thousands of imprisoned activists, documenting the abuses of the "bezpieka" (secret police) and arranging and redistributing the material help from abroad. These were tasks through which their invisibility was, if I may say, doubled by the fact that all of this work was illegal. It was a form of housework, but directed at the common good; personal involvement, but in public matters—a form of public involvement. This clearly escapes classical notions of the public sphere,

---

* During an art project at the Gdańsk shipyard in 2004, I conducted interviews with the women working there, some of whom were already employed in 1980. Their memories were bitter, as their hopes for a better situation for workers and women had clearly been betrayed in the economic transformation of the nineties. The main thesis of David Ost's book *The Defeat of Solidarity,* published in 2005—that Solidarność actually abandoned the workers and turned against them in building the new capitalist society after 1989—was broadly confirmed by my interviews. In 2004, facing their precarization in the labor market, these women were sometimes working three shifts consecutively and risking accidents. They were not active in unions because apart from the overload of paid work at the shipyard, they also had unpaid housework to do. Their families often depended on them financially yet the traditional gender division of labor continued in their homes. While men working in the shipyard always had time to sit down and talk with my friend, artist Iwona Zając, after their work to discuss their work situation, it was much harder to have meaningful discussions with women workers, whom I was interviewing, given their time constraints. They were only available during their short lunch breaks, or in the mornings when they were changing for work, or in the evenings as they were preparing to leave the shipyard. As a result of conversations unfolding through quick chats, my interviews took some three weeks altogether. Also, I am unaware of any journalist interviewing women in the shipyard either before or after my visit, which explains some aspects of the women's invisibility. This is gender inequality in practice.

such as the one proposed by Habermas, and maybe it could be seen as some form of counterpublic in the sense given to this formation by Fraser or Kluge, but as a hybrid and not monolithic entity.[60]

Feminist authors point to the fact that affective and care labor occupying women's time and energy, forcing the alienation and exploitation of women even today, constitutes a necessary element in the system of capitalist production. Domestic labor is not only exploitative, as Mariarosa Dalla Costa, Silvia Federici and other feminists have argued;[61] it is also a way of sharing a life with others, as has been depicted in the work of bell hooks. We can even think of it in terms of "love power," like the kind argued for by Anna Jónasdóttir over the last thirty years.[62] Solidarność made at least three *explicit* stipulations to support women in the twenty-one demands of the workers' unions in 1980: retirement age for women should be fifty; a three-year paid maternity leave; and enough daycare centers for all children. As a movement, however, Gdańsk failed to comprehend the degree of structural gender inequalities, and I believe this is a reason for the later exclusion of women from its ranks and programs. This basic incomprehension not only resulted in the conservative turn of the movement but also in the political parties that originated from it. Together these forces conspired to ignore and hence neglect women's issues in Polish politics after 1989.

We can reduce Solidarność to a sexist, misogynist entity altogether, as has often been done. But before doing so, we may want to examine how women were actually active there—otherwise our critique of misogyny will add to the erasure of women's political agency from historical accounts. We may also want to compare this particular movement with other social movements of the time in order to understand how and whether it differed from them in its gender bias. Interestingly, the outcome of this comparison is surprisingly positive for Solidarność. The trio of working-class female leaders of the August 1980 strike—crane operator Anna Walentynowicz, nurse Alina Pienkowska and tramway driver Henryka Krzywonos—were recognized by the movement, as were other women, including Solidarność expert Jadwiga Staniszkis, journalists/authors Helena Łuczywo and Joanna Szczęsna, activists like Barbara Labuda (probably the only *declared* feminist in the movement in 1980) and Joanna Duda-Gwiazda, who was one of the key negotiators of the August Agreements, and lawyers Zofia Wasilkowska and Janina Zakrzewska. These are just some examples of women who not only did important work, but were known in 1980 and are remembered today.

Just for comparison: how many women do we know from working-class resistance at the time of Thatcher's neoliberal takeovers in the early 1980s in England, the free-speech movement in the United States or the anti-apartheid mobilizations in South Africa? Or in the French student mobilizations of the 1960s? Probably no more than in Solidarność—and I emphasize this not because I would like to idealize this particular counterpublic, but because I think its social and academic perception should be built in comparison with other political mobilizations of the time and judged accordingly, not just to the scarce documentation of women's presence, but also to the general standards of the time, which were far more exclusive than they are today. Perhaps Solidarność should be blamed for its exclusions; however, when it comes to the years 1980 and 1981, it is mostly historians who omitted women, thus erasing them from the collective memory.

Another comparison that should be drawn if Solidarność is to be judged correctly from a feminist perspective concerns the state apparatus in Poland at the time. In 1980, women did not occupy important positions in state institutions. They were decorative elements of the ministerial salons. Women's participation in the Parliament of the "People's Republic of Poland" varied from 4 to 14 percent in the late 1950s to 25 percent after the 1980 elections. In the first days of Solidarność, many of the broader international legal guarantees of gender equality were not yet ready. The UN Beijing Declaration, probably the most famous and all-encompassing document concerning the rights of women and girls, was not even written in 1980 and it was only signed in 1995. The UN Convention on the Elimination of All Forms of Discrimination Against Women (CEDAW) was adopted in 1979 and signed by Poland in 1980. I believe that it was actually the result of signing this convention that women's participation in

Parliament in 1980 jumped to the previously unseen level of 25 percent.

The fact that we still know and remember the names of some women active at the core of Solidarność is, in my view, due to the more general democratization of the public sphere in 1980 in Poland—a moment that serves as a great example of the "mésentente" (disagreement) of Jacques Rancière. The appearance of the nurse, the female crane operator and the female tramway driver was, as we might say according to Rancière, a "new division of the sensible."[63] It was a sign and a declaration for the entire society that women do engage politically. The fact that perhaps more feminist writing has been dedicated to the (in-)famous slogan on the wall of the Gdańsk shipyard, *Kobiety, nie przeszkadzajcie nam walczyć o Polskę* ("Women, do not disturb our fight for Poland") than to some women actually involved in Solidarność is shameful proof of these women's lack of recognition rather than documentation of scientific and historical accuracy in Polish studies of that period. The performative dimension of this sudden presence of women cannot be reduced to an "exception" and pacified as "accidental." It was a genuine element of the early days of Solidarność and should be analyzed as an example of the unprecedented political mobilization of women, especially of the working class. As Małgorzata Tarasiewicz estimates in an interview concerning the "Women's Section" of Solidarność, women constituted approximately 50 percent of the movement.[64]

The invisibility of women's labor has been a major obstacle to women's political participation and involvement, both in the past and now. The substantial expropriation of its value is made possible by the affective involvement of those providing such labor; another contributory factor is the gendered character of the division of labor into productive and reproductive roles. While the latter has been pushed to the private domain and kept unpaid for centuries, it assisted in the reproduction of the species, as Marx and Engels depict it, and thus needs to be reevaluated today, when some parts of it are commercialized and some parts of the feminist movement openly demand its monetarization, as exemplified by the Wages for Housework movement of the 1970s. Reproductive labor should be reduced neither to its material results nor to the supposed "immateriality" of its affective practice, since affection, as contemporary studies rightly show, is neither immaterial nor independent of the social.* This labor does, however, have strong emancipatory potential for those who decide to unlearn privilege, who not only claim but also practice equality. From the perspective of reducing women's rights within the neoliberal transformation and its cuts to social services and support, the engagement of women in Solidarność might be seen as a version of Lauren Berlant's cruel optimism, an attachment to the object that was supposed to lead to happiness, yet eventually became an obstacle in this pursuit.[65] But on the other hand, we might also claim that this involvement is a lesson of the necessity to build feminist historiography beyond public/private divides, open to account not just for the most heroic and visible agents, but also those whose political agency consists of non-heroic, weak and ordinary resistance.

---

* Here I refer to the concept of "immaterial labor," promoted by Hardt and Negri in their earlier books, *Empire* and *Multitude*. It is worth noting that in *Commonwealth* they discuss "biopolitical labor," clearly the result of feminist and Marxist critiques of their previous terminology. See Michael Hardt and Antonio Negri, *Empire*, Cambridge: Harvard University Press, 2000 and *Multitude: War and Democracy in the Age of Empire*, New York: Penguin Press, 2004.

2

Feminist Counterpublics:
From Ophelia to Current Women's Protests

*After becoming a Category 2 hurricane and fluctuating in intensity
for a day, Ophelia intensified into a major hurricane on 14 October
south of the Azores, brushing the archipelago with high winds and
heavy rainfall. Shortly after achieving peak intensity, Ophelia began
weakening as it accelerated over progressively colder waters to its
northeast towards Ireland and Great Britain.*

"Hurricane Ophelia," Wikipedia

*I am always amazed by it. Encore! . . . What has favoured me for some
time is that there is apparently also on your part, in the great mass
of you, who are here, the same I don't want to know anything about
it . . . I am leaving you then on this bed, to your own inspiration.*

Jaques Lacan, *Séminaire XX*

The Young-Girl is crazy about the authentic because it's a lie.

Tiqqun, *Preliminary Materials for a Theory of the Young-Girl*

In this chapter I discuss women's entry into the public sphere and
some visions for the future.[1] I begin with a reference to Ophelia, a
symbolic figure usually classified as a "victim of unhappy love";
however, for me she symbolizes women's exclusion from the public
sphere and from culture in general. I then discuss Nancy Fraser's
concept of feminist counterpublics, suggesting a shift towards "subaltern counterpublics," which she defined—however, she somehow
later left it aside—and which I believe allows for interesting generalization about various counterpublics of the excluded, embracing

postcolonial as well as gender politics. I also present the current feminist protests since 2016, in Poland, as well as the International Women's Strike globally, as feminist counterpublics. I argue that we should see these women's mobilizations, as well as campaigns such as #MeToo, as core elements of contemporary politics, not merely in its margins. The brief discussion of social reproduction theory offered herein explains how a theoretical shift within feminist politics also translated into the popularity of recent feminist mobilization; I even argue that this feminist materialism actually allowed for the recognition of both reproductive rights and the need for freedom from gender-based violence as problems of society as a whole, not merely specific to some groups. In this chapter I also revisit Antigone—inspired by Bonnie Honig and her book *Antigone, Interrupted,* which offers a feminist reinterpretation of her relation with Ismene as an "antipatriarchal, sororal pact." I likewise discuss the efforts to bring feminism to academia—as a workplace, it is an important place for feminism to be practiced, not solely theorized. I discuss Sara Ahmed's diversity work, as well as my own academic activism against discrimination, in the larger context of feminist counterpublics.

The recent feminist protests prove that the hegemony of white, straight, privileged masculinity in the antifascist resistance is over; the time has come for us to learn to depict antifascism as feminist and antiracist. Specifically, the assault on reproductive rights in so many countries today constitutes an element of necropolitics, which forces women to embrace the heroic fate of confronting death in order to be dignified as citizens. The notion of "necropolitics" was created by Achille Mbembe, whose important work I reference later. In further parts of this book, I return to the issue of media and feminism, as well as weak resistance as a proposition for antifascist, left, progressive politics today. Here I focus on feminist counterpublics, which I understand as prioritizing women and LGBTQ+ persons without imposing any exclusive, essentializing notions as to what either of the groups enumerated here might be.˙

---

* I need to emphasize that these notions of women and femininity should not be read in an essentializing way. The majority of protests I depict here are

As we enter Zorka Wollny's highly theatrical performance of *Ophelias: Iconography of Madness*, in which we are surrounded by eleven actresses of different ages (between age twenty-five and eighty) and performative traditions, all playing the role of Ophelia, we find ourselves at the center of women's distress, women's pain and women's madness.[2] As we participate in this action, it brings together the polyphonic sounds of insane women. We hear splinters of wounded love discourse tossed around, which we know will become a shroud for an abandoned girl who throws herself into the water. The clash between two formats—performance (a free, spontaneous action generated by human bodies at a museum or gallery) and theater, regulated by a script (a classic!), acting methods, direction, dramaturgy and stage design—intensifies the already paralyzing women's madness. There is not just one Ophelia, but many: eleven women of different ages, whose acting follows different conventions, sometimes interacting with the audience, while at other times staying at a consciously kept distance. Each of them had played Ophelia earlier, but in a different theater, in a different decade and style. They sometimes look like the hysterics in photographs from the Salpêtrière clinic, and other times they're ordinary women like you and me. They

caused by or connected to reproductive rights; however, I am against limiting them to "women" or limit by any restrictive, exclusive and transphobic or otherwise essentialist categories. "Women" is a category that remains necessary. However, it is insufficient to discuss feminist politics today; it has to be shifted due to the needs and struggles of persons and communities living alternative embodiments and social lives to those shaped by binary gender codes. It also needs rethinking in this time of radical deconstruction of binary genders and sexual identities, as well as in recognition of the long and painful struggles the LGBTQI+ persons have endured in the past. In recognition of this necessary transformation, I sometimes say: women and LGBTQI+ persons; however, this is also a problematic shift, as it somehow poses a difference between women and lesbians or transgender people that is not always welcomed, although some people actually embrace it. Also, reproductive rights are also about some straight men. I am sure we need a more revolutionary discursive practice than the one I can offer in this book; however, as I cannot pursue it here, I just try to avoid the most obvious traps of heteronormativity while trying to combine gender insubordinations and comprehensive narrative.

are everywhere. They are walking, sitting, standing, bending their bodies, making a "hysteric's" bridge, animating, withdrawing, howling, whispering and screaming, sometimes uttering words, or simply letting out terrible noises.

European culture does not usually welcome transgressions of rigid rules of womanhood, defined as valiant and submissive. This absence is emphasized by the author of *Antigone, Interrupted*, Bonnie Honig, whose moving reconstruction of Sophocles's tragedy draws attention to the hitherto unnoticed alliance between Ismene and Antigone— figures whom most critics consider apart. According to Honig, in their collusion, "one would not move forward without the other."[3] In *Hamlet* as well as in Wollny's performance, Ophelia is alone (although multiplied), surrounded by politicians and the world of men as well as her half-conscious loved one, Hamlet, who, with a fragile male ego, is incapable, of course, of going beyond predictable liberal individualism because his role is to act out the drama of the modern "self" formed among monarchies and plantations. The role of Ophelia—a clever and poetic girl, but also a hostage to her gender role and the culture imposing it, a femininity that is fragile and vulnerable—is to act out madness, rooted in separation. She is a perfect supporting character who only amplifies the affective turmoil experienced by the protagonist. She is his shadow and the unknown (and never to be known) embodiment of mad passion limited to the intellect, an embodied supplement, whose sensuality and body tossing itself around the stage complement the intellectual-political expression of power formed in cruelty and violence. In *Capital*, Karl Marx wrote about the dispossessed, that "the history of their expropriation is written in the annals of mankind in letters of blood and fire."[4] In the case of Ophelia, her own expropriation from life proceeds by kinder methods of gendered norms and stereotypes; however, this also has dramatic consequences.

In confronting Antigone, Creon accuses her of imposing on the state and civilization a disorder that is characteristic of women. These words, almost literally repeated by Rousseau, are analyzed from a feminist perspective by Carole Pateman, who rightly emphasizes the depth of male fear about the confusion, transgression and affect that women supposedly bring into public spheres.[5] Pateman is one of those authors who lays bare, with extreme dynamism and precision, the division—problematic from women's perspective—into private and public spheres, which lies at the core of liberal and conservative political theory. For this reason, her feminist analysis of the "fraternal social contract"—which underpins liberal democracies and consists of reenacting the king's authoritarian power not over his sons, as it was under absolutism, but over women—is interwoven with socialist critiques of liberal democracy that highlight the exclusion of those involved in production (the workers) from their rights and political institutions. I find this analogy—between affect and production, workers and women—to be productive and have traction in discussions pursued in the field of aesthetics and including debates on *Hamlet* and the character of Ophelia.

Such discussion also presupposes a certain potentially non-individualistic horizon, the possibility of perceiving humans in a relational and contextual manner—without separation. It presupposes Ophelia's exit from isolation and invisibility as well as an invasion—committed by her, her experiences, her words, the world of her mind and her madness—of the structure of existing culture. It seems that this is exactly what Wollny manages to achieve. In her artwork we witness not only a performance of eleven hysterics liberated from the tragedy of the Danish kingdom, but also, more broadly, we examine the significance of their appearance in public—intensified, multiplied and staged. The performative seriality of Wollny's *Ophelias*, as well as their multiplication by age and by dramaturgic styles, costumes and forms of interaction with the audience, all turn the performance into a participatory piece, where the audience involuntarily reenacts the silencing mechanisms of the public sphere. Various girlish ways of having fun—panicking, rising, falling, fearing, and other affective idioms—are enacted many times, in various styles and by very different women. This brings to mind Hélène Cixous's classic manifesto *The Laugh of the Medusa*, in which femininity is portrayed as repressed by male-dominated culture, yet it nevertheless claims access to this culture. Cixous writes:

Beauty will no longer be forbidden. I wish that that woman would write and proclaim this unique empire, so that other women, other unacknowledged sovereigns, might exclaim: I, too, overflow; my desires have invented new desires, my body knows unheard-of songs. Time and again I, too, have felt so full of luminous torrents that I could burst—burst with forms much more beautiful than those which are put up in frames and sold for a stinking fortune. And I, too, said nothing, showed nothing; I didn't open my mouth, I didn't repaint my half of the world. I was ashamed. I was afraid, and I swallowed my shame and my fear. I said to myself: You are mad! What's the meaning of these waves, these floods, these outbursts?[6]

This is how Ophelia would likely have spoken if she had had the opportunity and ability to speak, if her jump into the river had somehow been prevented. We may attempt to read Ophelia with the tools proposed by Gayatri Spivak—as a "subaltern," deprived of voice in patriarchal culture, as someone whose voice is always already entangled in patriarchal catachresis, regulating her exceptionality through the demands of the accepted perception of "people like her" by the dominant groups.[7] We also situate and contextualize Ophelia depending on the circumstances, regarding her as rejected, mad, hysterical. Elaine Showalter underlines that this indeed happens devastatingly often: "Though she is neglected in criticism, Ophelia is probably the most frequently illustrated and cited of Shakespeare's heroines."[8] Concentrating on the question of Ophelia's representation, Showalter somehow pacifies her agency, although she intentionally performs a feminist reading. By strictly separating the experience of contemporary women from the figure, character or role of Ophelia, she effectively stabilizes her as an object of exclusion, which is exactly the opposite of what Wollny does by not only bringing Ophelia to life and extracting her from the context of Shakespeare's play, but also by multiplying and enriching her. In Showalter's analysis, Ophelia is frozen in her impossibility, exclusion and helplessness. She is discussed like a museum piece of representation: bygone, absent and, in a certain sense, impossible. What indeed makes the figure of Ophelia so terribly moving, especially for contemporary women, are these elements of her madness and distress, which form parts of our own experience of patriarchal culture. For this very reason, it is not only through historical precision—as much as it also characterizes Wollny's work—that her "presentation" of Ophelia can turn into a tool of political representation.

Ophelia is a figure of loss—the loss of balance, security, life. She is a weak and volatile figure, but also one that can be seen as banal and repetitive, which makes her somewhat familiar and common. Howling, throwing flowers or uttering inarticulate whispers, Ophelia is a foreign body in the landscape of liberal democracy, not a subject with agency. In order to talk about her in any depth, one needs to challenge the entire paradigm of patriarchal culture, as was done by Linda Nochlin. In 1971, Nochlin dismantled the very premise of the question "Why have there been no great women artists?" by asking: For whom is the system of political represent-ation designed?[9] How does it accommodate people from outside dominant groups and what mechanisms of domination are imposed on them almost immediately when they attempt to make their voices heard in this system?

In the actions of the Ophelias staged by Wollny, we observe not only the workings of the system of artistic presentation, but we also experience the problems and limitations of political represent-ation. We find in ourselves and in others all those abandoned, ridiculed, isolated and distressed women for whom the experience of confrontation with traditional gender norms is akin to a clash with an adversary that they cannot combat. The Ophelias invite us to work against separation by imposing on the audience the experi-ences of exclusion, rejection and dissent. As we look at them, we may begin the performance of our own affective memory, in which our own experience of trauma or rejection will be acted out, but also perhaps worked through. Looking at the Ophelias, we are a bit similar to Chloe looking at Olivia in Virginia Woolf's *A Room of One's Own*: we like her. And then we realize how seldom we look at women in an unmediated way in the realm of a male-centric culture.

According to Alexander Kluge and Oskar Negt, counterpublics are critical for the authorities and the existing elites as spaces of public debate and political agency. As I have explained in the previous chapter, Kluge and Negt do not abandon the problematic of production but situate it at the heart of their theory of a counter public sphere. As opposed to Habermas's bourgeois public sphere, counterpublics are proletarian and they problematize the lived experience of producers—workers. In a much later text, the topic of counterpublics was addressed again by feminist philosopher Nancy Fraser, who proposes the category of feminist counterpublics as an example of a public that escapes the limitations of Habermas's concept.[10] Feminist counterpublics move across the division that splits the public and private into distinct spheres, which is of key importance to Habermas and, more generally, to liberal democracies; in Fraser's formulation, it is polyvocal and heterogeneous. Exactly like the Ophelias in Wollny's work, feminist counterpublics operate on various registers and intervene in various parts of patriarchal culture. They diagnose its exclusions and marginalizations, articulate violence and madness, while their interaction with the audience generates a frame for broad debate about the (non-)presence of women in culture and politics, thus opening up critical possibilities.

In "Rethinking the Public Sphere," Fraser claims that Habermas's theory solves the conflation of three registers: "the state, the official economy of paid employment, and arenas of public discourse."[11] She is correct to point out that in feminist debates, but also more generally, these registers are confused with the public sphere. I would add to this the notion of "public space," which is often entangled with the public sphere. Lack of clarity around their distinction can sometimes lead to the presumption that it is enough to exhibit something outside for it to qualify as public art.[12] Fraser agrees that the idea of the public sphere can be as useful for democratic politics as it is for critical theory. Yet she does not accept certain basic elements of Habermas's approach. She therefore enumerates four main problems of Habermas's concept of the public sphere that make it a "masculinist bourgeois" theory and therefore unacceptable, namely: the belief that social differences of status can be bracketed off; the assumption that multiplicity at the core of the public sphere would endanger its genuine character; the belief that any appearance of private or particular matters would destroy the public sphere; and the sense of necessary division between the social and the state.

These masculinist bourgeois conditions of Habermas's public sphere are obviously grounded in the core assumption that the public/private division is fundamental and necessary for the public sphere. Fraser argues, against Habermas, that the normative criteria of discursive agency in contemporary societies depend on gender and material status, and they should therefore be negotiated. Moreover, this should be conducted within the public sphere itself—and hence it bypasses its framework. Fraser writes about "subaltern counterpublics" and as her main example, she takes "subaltern feminist counterpublics." While this strikes me as a brilliant idea, it should have been done with more attention to postcolonial theory and the problems of the structural persistence of colonial and racist exclusions. We can think, for instance, of work by Spivak and other theorists that would be exceptionally useful in this regard. Fraser's subaltern counterpublics are those that openly negotiate the division into public and private spheres. She mentions that men tend to interrupt women much more often than women interrupt men, but this instance should, in my opinion, be seen as the beginning of a much longer list of problems that women have to face in public.[13] I have already mentioned Pateman's theory of the fraternal social contract. Here I would simply remind readers that in her view, the basic problem of gender in the public sphere is the structural discrimination against women in society. This starts very early and is perpetrated throughout our lives in major institutions, by relatives, friends and partners, on every level of our existence. You will recall that some 30 percent of women suffer domestic violence, and almost 50 percent of women have survived attempts of rape at least once in their lifetime. All these experiences influence the lives of women, and LGBTQ+ persons as well, given that some of these groups sometimes suffer even more violence.

Fraser depicts feminist counterpublics as sites of critical debate that actively transform politics. She claims:

In general, critical theory needs to take a harder, more critical look at the terms "private" and "public." These terms, after all, are not simply straightforward designations of societal spheres; they are cultural classifications and rhetorical labels. In political discourse, they are powerful terms that are frequently deployed to delegitimate some interests, views, and topics and to valorize others.[14]

Fraser's essay was published thirty years ago, but her words and thinking are only beginning to gain visibility today. This is thanks in no small part to the women's protests, the constant activity of feminist groups, scholars and organizations and such campaigns as #MeToo. On the left, the issue of public/private has been neglected because, on one hand, "everyone is a feminist" today; and on the other, this division has permeated our fundamental understanding of politics, and therefore it will not go away when we say "psik" (or whatever people say in English when they want a cat to move).

The women's protests in Poland since 2016 have built a transversal movement.[15] They explore patterns of resistance through various forms and styles, old and new, as they reference the nineteenth-century women's protests (hence the black clothes); the women's strike, inspired by the 1975 women's strike in Iceland, but also by the Polish strikes of 1905, 1971 and 1980, where women were particularly active, as well as the 2007 "White Protests" of the nurses.[16] They have also used social media and networking, organizing in ways inspired by Solidarność, the legendary workers' union. To my mind, this connection between reproductive rights and labor successfully deflated the myth that feminism is a solely middle-class movement.

Before 2016, women's and feminist organizations existed in Poland, and they sometimes gained great visibility. There are at least ten gender studies programs in various Polish universities, and some thousand registered non-governmental organizations at least mentioning the rights of women in their programs. The feminist movement has been very vocal in the last twenty years, engaging with abortion and reproductive politics, violence against women, politics, labor, culture and other spheres. However, the majority of registered and grassroots organizations are located in big cities or towns, and their members often belong to the urban, educated middle class.

As the 2016 women's protests began as a reaction to the bills restricting the already harsh antiabortion Polish law, I need to offer some highlights of the reproductive rights battles as well as those more generally concerning gender. Under Poland's current law, abortion is legal only in three cases: when the pregnancy was the result of rape; when the fetus shows risks of severe damage or illness; or when the life of the woman is endangered. Unfortunately, even under these conditions women often do not obtain permission to terminate their pregnancies, usually because of the doctor's convictions, which generally leads them either to illegal abortions, in Poland or abroad, or to risk their lives/health and give birth.[17] The bill, against which the Black Protests have been held since 2016, would make abortion completely illegal and would allow authorities to sentence women to prison for up to two years. Currently it is only those who help women access abortions who can be accused of breaking the law, but it almost never happens.

I want to emphasize the necropolitical aspect of the antiabortion campaigns and legal proposals that have been presented since 2016. In October 2016, the head of the Conservative Party (PiS), Jarosław Kaczyński, declared: "We want women to give birth even in cases when the child is deformed. We want such children to be baptized, buried, to have a name."[18] There was wide media commentary on this statement, effectively spreading panic among women. Kaczyński's declaration clearly places the life of the fetus above the life, health and well-being of the woman. It also suggests that in discussions about pregnancy, women can be omitted; we can be stripped of any rights, presence or even visibility. The panic resulting from this particular statement was backed up by the fact that since 2015, Kaczyński's party has had a parliamentary majority. This means PiS (Prawo i Sprawiedliwość) could—with the support of right-wing allies, but also with the votes of some supposed liberals who are actually conservative—change the law and make abortion completely illegal.

There are different definitions of power, as Mbembe writes: "The ultimate expression of sovereignty resides, to a large degree, in the power and the capacity to dictate who may live and who must die."[19] We know this definition of power all too well, from Carl Schmitt's obsessive conceptualizations of the sovereign and from Jean Bodin and his admiration for the figure of *pater familias*. We know the political and historical heritages of those conceptual frameworks, and we want them to never happen again. In Mbembe's philosophical project, the sovereign's power over life and death is tangible, the biopolitical is intertwined with the carceral, and the depictions of perverse power over the lives of individual people are sensory and painful. And this is the pain that we also felt in Poland while listening to Kaczyński's previously stated declaration concerning abortion. Interestingly, Kaczyński's brother, Lech, the former president of Poland who died in a plane crash in 2010, employed Carl Schmitt's translator as one of his main advisors between 2005 and 2010. This could be seen as accidental; however, PiS politics strikingly resemble the Schmittian doctrine of the state of exception, on many levels, including the subjugation of justice by the executive powers of the state (the minister of justice and the president are currently above all judicial institutions). Women's subjugation seems like a parallel transition.

In the Schmittian politics of the state of exception, the sovereign is above the law while remaining as the only one allowed to change it. Such political doctrine was central in German fascism of the 1930s, and we now see crucial elements of it enacted in Poland, a country inhabited by a population the Nazis saw as "under-humans" (*untermenschen*). The notion of the state of exception in Schmitt's narrative can only operate if combined with the corresponding notion of the enemy, who has to be clearly designated, stripped of their political power, rights, property and eventually also life. In Nazi Germany, Jews, Romani, Sinti, communists, gay men and some other groups were positioned as such enemies, while in today's Poland this position has already been occupied by refugees, LGBTQ+ people, and now also women. In the 2015 electoral campaign, members of the PiS party compared refugees with rats and insects—they blamed them for spreading contagious diseases and for causing higher unemployment. All these arguments had already been used by the Nazis against Jews

in the 1930s.[20] Now the local and regional authorities in some 25
percent of the regions of Poland voted for these laws, which directly or
indirectly exclude LGBTQ+ people. A European Parliament resolution
was voted on to protest these laws, which abound in southeast Poland
and have unfortunately spread. These laws are supposedly "harmless"—
as some PiS authorities declare, they do not contain any executive
resolutions. However, as discrimination can be caused by singling out
particular groups, LGBTQ+ persons have very solid claims against
such laws, and they were backed up by the Polish Ombudsman, who,
also in December 2019, sued several local governments for crossing
their legal competences by installing such laws.

There is, however, another aspect of the politics of the state of
exception that needs to be emphasized. In the fascist state of exception, everyone has to be a hero—only the enemy is perceived as weak.
We should imagine Carl Schmitt's "partisan" as accompanied by the
heroic Mother of Many, one depicted as "asexual and holy" in Klaus
Theweleit's *Male Fantasies*.[21] This Mother of Many cannot discuss,
negotiate or change her condition. The caring hand of the sovereign
has direct access to her body. She is treated as a national resource and
for this reason, she is stripped of her constitutive rights, as well as
dehumanized; she can even be sacrificed for the greater good of the
nation, which here is understood as expanding the population.

The often-neglected symmetry between women's and men's absolute subjection to unmediated sovereign power in the doctrine of the
state of exception is crucial to understanding how the reproductive
rights and restrictions of civil rights and liberties constitute two sides
of the same coin of contemporary fascisms. Both men and women are
forced to embrace the heroic role of a mother, or a soldier, against all
costs and risks. This points to the assumption, at least in Poland, that
women should constitute themselves as subjects by confronting death.
Apparently, men constitute themselves as subjects by merely existing,
or being declared patriots, but women need to be confronted with the
actual risk of death to become citizens. It is a mistake of Giorgio
Agamben, otherwise a great theorist of the state of exception, to omit
the problem of gender and women in his account of Schmitt's doctrine
and its contemporary repercussions. This problem has been pointed

out by Spivak and Judith Butler in their book *Who Sings the Nation-State?* They undermine the passivity of *homo sacer* in Agamben's theory of sovereignty, and rightly so.[22] As they observe, the gender of this important figure is tacitly assumed to be masculine. They do not emphasize enough, I believe, that the misogynist politics they rightly criticize rely on the systematic denial of reproductive rights as an element of the state of exception doctrine. In a similar vein, the omission of reproductive rights in contemporary critiques of fascism strikes me as a major mistake of progressive political theories. As clearly evidenced by the women's protests in Poland and globally, these particular rights are at the heart of democratic politics.

The ease with which even feminist political theorists ignore the significance of reproductive rights as core to democratic politics is, I believe, a repercussion of the persistence of the private/public division in political theory and practice. We are not used to seeing reproductive rights as crucial to democracy, as we only seldom see topics classified as "private" entering the public debate. Yet we must, or else we risk perpetuating a fascist state of exception for minorities and women. Feminist authors, from Pateman to Fraser, as well as some critical theorists, who openly discuss—as Axel Honneth does—the influence of violence experienced in private lives on the possibility of claims to recognition further prove the importance of the end of the traditional division between public and private spheres.[23]

If fundamental reproductive rights are limited, questioned or denied, democratic participation is unequally distributed, which results in disproportionate access to various activities, including committing time and energy for political involvement and the dignity necessary for the execution of political rights. Due to the fact that feminist activists have fought for abortion and won this battle in most countries in the West, while state communism introduced it in the East—with exceptions, but also in Poland (a fascinating story in itself, how abortion rights have changed in the USSR since 1919)—we almost forgot that for some decades in the nineteenth and early twentieth centuries, women were banned from terminating their pregnancies and still are in so many countries in the world. With the astonishing US Supreme Court nominations of 2018, we might expect abortion rights to be revisited and challenged in that country. In Italy, the city of Verona suddenly declared itself a "pro-life city" in October 2018, and more surprises of this kind are on the way. The so-called gender wars in European countries and the global online antifeminist backlash further prove the importance of reproductive rights, somehow assumed to be granted.[24]

The massive participation of women in demonstrations since 2016 was also fueled by the campaigns of hate speech against feminism and women, coming from various conservative politicians and high-ranking representatives of the Catholic Church. Elżbieta Korolczuk, Agnieszka Graff and other feminist scholars argue that this retaliation has been building in Polish and other European media, public debate and parliaments since at least 2013.[25] The "gender wars," which have been strongly supported by conservative Parliament members such as Krystyna Pawłowicz (a member of the ruling PiS party), have smeared the names of several good journalists, resulting in her being sentenced for hate speech and related offenses. Of course, this situation is not particular to Poland; similar movements have been seen in France and Italy, where demonstrations were held "against the ideology of gender." However, in Poland, this war on feminism transformed into a mass media campaign against the basic rights of women, our dignity and well-being. Unfortunately, this was accompanied by actual procedural transformations of medical assistance for pregnant women, reducing their rights to decide on procedures, limiting prenatal exams of the fetus and otherwise limiting these women's access to health care. Women were obviously infuriated with this situation, even before the antiabortion bill was introduced, so when it was announced, it seemed like a trigger to an already loaded gun.

Mobilizing women against further restrictions on abortion began in early 2016, first in preexisting women's and feminist organizations. After several years of hateful "gender wars" within a society where women still carry out the majority of care and affective labor, in April 2016 the Polish government announced a proposal to ban abortion completely.[26] Massive demonstrations spread across the country, unifying women across class, political persuasion and rural-urban divides under one general umbrella: that of women's rights and dignity.[27] Polish communities mobilized globally, and feminists from other countries joined in as well. As feminist groups in Italy, Mexico and Argentina were likewise planning demonstrations for fall 2016, mainly to protest violence against women, it was easy to network and combine the protests—and this is how the International Women's Strike began. Women in South Korea also protested in Seoul against the antiabortion laws in their country, using the Black Protest name and banners in solidarity with us in Poland. The women in the United States started their anti-Trump protests in winter 2016–17, and feminists from other countries, inspired by what was already happening, started to join, spreading the International Women's Strike to some seventy countries by 2018.

In April 2016, 100,000 women joined ad hoc Polish social media group Gals for Gals (Dziewuchy Dziewuchom) practically overnight. Local branches of this group started popping up as the protests developed, and from within these branches new leaders and activists appeared, often without any prior experience with activism and politics. The women's protests began that April, when, after just days of preparation, demonstrations in some fifty cities and towns took place, organized by women gathered in the Dziewuchy Dziewuchom groups, the older feminist organizations, and the Razem Party.

In September 2016, internet activism in support of women's rights and involving the #blackprotest hashtag and posting of black-and-white selfies online made it possible for countless women to actually engage in political protests. Many who demonstrated against the antiabortion bill in fall 2016 did so after "posting" their support online. Thus, for many women and LGBTQ+ people, as well as for some men, the "engaged selfie" and hashtag became an intermediary step between complete lack of involvement in politics and demonstrating in the streets. Clearly, this was a very powerful use of social media and the internet for the cause of the feminist protest. Moreover, it proved that social media actually *can* be used to mobilize and engage protestors, not just to appease them. This can also be an argument for "selfie-feminism," which in some part tends to follow a mainstream agenda; yet, in other cases, it effectively weakens and/or contradicts patriarchal abuse of women and LGBTQ+ people. Further online feminist actions, such as the #MeToo campaign and other hashtags, show how within internet cultural industries mainly aimed at profit, some solidarity, protest or resistance actions are nonetheless possible. I return to the topic of media in the next chapter, but I think it is worth signaling here that corporate communication capital can also be hijacked for better purposes, although never for long and never without causing backlash.

In September 2016, famous Polish actress Krystyna Janda declared that women should begin a strike, like in 1980, in response to the threat of the full ban on abortion. This statement became viral, and even the popular women's press started to write about the Women's Strike in Iceland in 1971 and other women's protests, thus making it "common" and "normal" for women to join protests. Janda is known from Andrzej Wajda's film *Człowiek z żelaza* (*Man of Iron*), mentioned in the previous chapter, as well as other movies, in which she plays nonconformist, oppositional female characters. Thus, as her statement strongly resonated and the association of women's contemporary protest and the early days of Solidarność started to circulate, it somehow legitimized the current need to protest as rooted in a distant yet appreciated moment of Poland's past.

This suggestion of striking introduced by Janda in the narrative of protest tacitly shifted the priorities of the feminist movement in 2016. The economy of reproductive labor, an invisible topic in the perspective established by liberal feminism on the abortion question—namely that focusing on choice—shifted toward the economy of the abortion ban, basically becoming another element of the sharpening class division between those who can and cannot afford abortion. Before 2016, it was quite difficult to discuss the economics of the abortion ban. Now, after discussions of women striking and how we understand it, it is very popular. This shift from the liberal preoccupation with "choice" toward a more socialist focus on the class composition of women as a group made the feminist narrative stronger and more compelling for the social masses. I believe this turn was crucial for mass participation in the protests.

The tensions between socialist/Marxist and liberal feminisms constitute an important part of the history of the women's movement, and they have been discussed elsewhere; thus, I will not reconstruct them in a wider analysis. It is crucial to note, however, that these controversies are somehow sublated in the contemporary feminist movement, which, through striking, resists from within the core of the social, mostly in the context of reproductive rights. The movement thus somehow opted for social reproduction theory (SRT), whether by choices the particular membership consciously made or not. To me, the popularity of the recent feminist protests shows the importance of SRT and the focus on reproduction it enforces.

A comprehensive introduction to SRT can be found in Tithi Bhattacharya's article "Mapping Social Reproduction Theory." It opens, as most feminist texts on reproduction, with a reference to the fundamental question—"Who produces the worker?"—already asked by Marx in his critique of political economy. This (re)production of the workforce covers various elements of what constitutes housework, affective labor and family; however, the notion of reproduction is perhaps the most general. Bhattacharya presents the origins of SRT as being the feminist preoccupation with the "silences" of Marxist narrative—the invisible labor of care, biological reproduction and maintaining social relations of kinship and beyond. The refusal to embrace these forms of agency as "work" deepens their exclusion and marginalization, thus translating into the diminished status of domestic workers—mainly women—in society. In her essay, Bhattacharya enumerates various classic Marxist feminist works, such as that of Lisa Vogel, as well as the more contemporary analysis of the Marxism-feminism debates, focusing on the issue of the problematic distinction between production and reproduction.[28]

The production of the exceptional commodity—the labor force or, to put it even more bluntly, humans—is most commonly excluded from money-mediated exchanges, and thus pushed out of the supposedly main Marxist focus on value production. However, as various currents of feminism rightly point out, especially in this time of cognitive capitalism and growing precarization, reproductive labor has become one of the central elements of capitalist production, as a form of work that is increasingly central to monetarized exchanges (as services and paid care work), as well as in its uniquity, caused, among other reasons, by the neoliberal withdrawal of states and employers from their responsibilities in health care and social services. As Italian feminists, including Laura Fantone and Silvia Federici, rightly claim, processes of precarization are far more demanding for women than for men, as—due to gendered socialization—women are seen as far more responsible for care and affective labor than men, and thus in times of the institutionalized dismantling of social security and health care, women end up with far more reproductive work than in previous decades. On the other hand, the evolution of capitalism toward service, tourism and entertainment fueled the massive incorporation of classical caring modes of behavior by the labor market. As Arlie Hochschild's classic 1979 study rightly points out, the "labor of the heart" is currently an important part of a vast number of professions. The work of hostesses and stewardesses constitutes the most renowned example. Through this shift, the prior invisibility of reproductive labor has been replaced with its immediate commodification. The Italian and American movement of "Wages for Housework" from the 1970s might see some parts of this transition as a realization of their demands, as, for instance, in Germany women who stay with their families and work at home are now entitled to retirement.

Before SRT, there were several approaches to the relations between Marxism and feminism, mainly focused, however, on their differences. Feminist standpoint theories, operaist feminism and Black feminism—just to name a few, and regardless of their differences—led to the general conclusion that Marxism provides the best tools to critique the political economy of housework. As various aspects of the social realm can be explained or at least critically addressed by the tools of SRT, reproduction became a key context in understanding the majority of social experiences, including those previously seen solely as aspects of intimate life or paid labor. The materialist feminism of SRT provides tools to understand various forms of exploitation and oppression in their relations to other parts of the capitalist economy. Earlier feminisms often separated them, thus creating an impression of the particularity of these experiences and thus supporting the problematic exclusivity of certain social issues, including those and abortion and domestic violence. Thus, as I suggested earlier, far more people have become involved in recent feminist protests and the materialist, concrete, historically contextualized explanation of the importance of reproductive rights or freedom from gender-based violence has finally started to be seen as valid, not merely a matter for women and LGBTQ+ persons.

Choosing the strike as a method of protest, women in Poland, as well as those in other countries who joined the International Women's Strike, emphasized that what was previously reduced to "choice" or exoticized and essentialized as a "women's problem" was in fact a social reproduction problem.

The #blackprotest social media campaign was initiated on September 23, 2016, by a member of the left-wing Razem Party, Gocha Adamczyk. Eventually it became the biggest thing on the Polish internet.[29] The idea was to post a black-and-white selfie together with the hashtag #blackprotest (#czarnyprotest). Between September 23 and 24, some 150,000 such selfies were posted online, while the hashtag #czarnyprotest was used some 8 million times on social media. On October 3, 2016, the day of the Women's Strike, that number rose to 53.7 million and demonstrations were held in some 150 cities and towns, with some 200,000 participants. Various groups of the Women's Strike—a grassroots feminist organization—started to spread across Poland and organize parallel demonstrations and marches, together with or sometimes separately from the Razem Party and other feminist groups. They most often formed following the Dziewuchy-Dziewuchom groups and constitute feminist networks "after 2016," which were notably diverse. Due to the international activism and travels of some of its members, including Klementyna Suchanow, the creation of the International Women's Strike was possible. Other members, such as Marta Lempart, struggled in Poland to gain visibility for the movement.

Adamczyk's simple yet powerful idea of the hashtag and selfie inspired women to join the protest and constituted an intermediary step between silence and a very loud street demonstration. The choice of the color black was simple: It is the traditional color of women's resistance in Poland and has been worn by widows as a practice of mourning since the mid-nineteenth century. This was at a time when commemorations of those killed or deported in and after the uprisings had been banned. In her article on political fashion in nineteenth-century Poland, Justyna Jaworska claims that in Warsaw around the year 1860, residents—both men and women—had to possess a document stating the reason for their black attire—that is, that it was justified by the death of a relative. Otherwise they would be punished by a fine or arrest.[30] The decision to promote black clothing as the uniform of the women's protests was also explained by its democratic possibilities, as many own clothes of this color. This proved far more successful than ever expected.

For most women, posting a selfie online from the September 23, 2016, #blackprotest action was a safe gesture. However, a group of teachers from Zabrze, a postindustrial town in Silesia, were reported to the Disciplinary Board of Education for posing in a picture of support for the Black Protests and posting it on social media. As the expression of political views is still legal in Poland, the board correctly deemed the complaint against the teachers unfounded. Nevertheless, the women endured many months of distress due to being reported by their male colleague, who clearly did not share their views.

On the day of the Women's Strike, October 3, 2016, there were heavy rains across Poland. As almost everyone had an umbrella, this has since become the symbol of the women's protests. We all wore black clothes, and some 150,000 women in Poland and abroad—in around 150 cities and towns—protested in the streets against the proposed draconian antiabortion law. Some wore black and went to work, but they published their support online. I have a very nice memory from right after the protest, with a group of friends, as we took a cab to go back home. In the car, we were discussing the protests, while the driver was silent. When it came to paying, it took some time for us to grab our purses, discuss who should pay what amount and so on. However, the driver simply said, "you pay nothing, thank you for being a part of this important protest, I fully embrace your cause." The protests succeeded in a more official way, too; the law was rejected in Parliament. In October 2020, however, the Constitutional Court made abortion illegal under almost any circumstances, including cases where the fetus suffered from severe disability or was unlikely to survive.

It is important that in the Black Protests and the Women's Strike, feminism ceased to be a movement of metropolitan women, not only on social media, but also in street protests. This was made possible by several strategic shifts—especially that from a liberal toward a socialist narrative, as well as that inviting women to somehow "rehearse" their political involvement over social media before taking it to the streets. For most women, it was safe to join the protests after they had already made the first step—the hashtag and the selfie were really effective this way. The charges of elitism, which feminists have endured since the early 1990s, have dissipated in recent years. Although certain liberal feminists still maintain their neglect of class inequality, the majority of the feminist movement's members, at least in Poland, correctly recognize the battle over reproduction as one where issues of gender and class intersect and cannot be discussed separately. The Black Protests made it very clear that the economic situation directly translates into gender inequality in the context of abortion, which has always been affordable and safe for some women regardless of restrictions, and it therefore should be legal, safe and state funded if equality is to be treated with due diligence.

The logo of the independent workers' union, Solidarność, was used by several participants in the Black Protests in 2016, including the one in Gdańsk. The protesters were accused by the current cowardly right-wing chiefs of Solidarność of breaching the union's ownership of the sign. The controversy included charges against Croatian artist Sanja Iveković, who, in 2009, transformed the Solidarność electoral poster from 1989 so that it depicted a woman instead of a man and the protestors sort of multiplied the women, adding several silhouettes instead of one and different shapes. The legendary cofounder of Solidarność, Henryka Krzywonos, fully supported the feminist protesters, joining them in demonstrations and declaring over social media her readiness to join them in jail if necessary. Eventually, the creator of the Solidarność logo, Jerzy Janiszewski, publicly declared that he allows everyone to use the design for their purposes, so long as they are progressive. And with this declaration, the controversy was over. The activists and artist were cleared of all charges in 2017.

There have been more women's protests since 2016. On March 8, 2017, tens of thousands of Polish women participated in the International Women's Strike, together with women in at least fifty other countries. Another International Women's Strike took place a year later, on March 8, 2018, and people in sixty countries participated.[31] An additional massive protest in Poland took place on March 23, 2018; dubbed "Black Friday," it was convened when the government again discussed a law banning abortion. Some 90,000 women and supporters marched in the streets of Warsaw alone, and another 60,000 in other cities and towns. We can well expect further protests, as the abortion law remains an important topic in public debate. Many Polish women also joined the International Women's Strike, connecting dissent in Poland with women's protests globally.[32]

The women's protests have been the most successful political resistance against Poland's current government since 2015; in fact, all others have lost significant ground. Although there have been some restrictions on women's rights in the medical sector, the movement is still seen as the only one that effectively resisted and stopped Kaczynski's party. It therefore changed the position of women in Polish society and had a strong impact on women's representation in media and science. Any misrepresentation or lack of gender balance is currently harshly criticized and, if possible, changed. The women's protests also gained the attention of political parties, with all of them appealing to women for obvious reasons. These changes are unfortunately fading with further negative transformation of the laws and political practices in Poland, with almost every sector of public life being governed either by conservatives with fascist tendencies or by liberal economic elites, who—when it comes to women—often do not present themselves as very different than their right-wing counterparts. Due to this twofold opposition, the women's protests should be seen as a "feminist counterpublic," as depicted in Nancy Fraser's seminal essay.[33] On the one hand, the protests are against the ruling conservative party; on the other, this resistance is against the values that are likewise fundamental for liberal elites of the political opposition.

In her seminal book *Gender Trouble*, a study on the social and cultural shaping of gender, Judith Butler emphasizes the symbolic and physical violence resulting from the patriarchal reaction of heteronormative society to people who transgress the binary codes of gender and sexual orientation.[34] I have always been tempted to verify how that works in the context of the public sphere with regard to women and LGBTQ+ persons who fully or partially embody the social practice of "femininity." What happens to a woman, or a person who does not identify as such yet assumes the "feminine" position, when they try to enter the public realm? What does women's presence in the public sphere look like? What happens to women who attempt to participate in public debate?

Some of this deconstructive work has already been done. In the groundbreaking essay "The Laugh of the Medusa," Cixous emphasizes the exceptionality of women's public presentation, which she herself experienced in the 1960s and 1970s.[35] Yet by the sheer fact of women entering various public institutions and professions, we tend to forget how exceptional it still is for women to be public. The language is not helpful here, as it denotes a very different meaning to a "public woman" from that it assigns to the idiom "public man." As distant as we might feel from the emotional depiction of the public speech of the subject in "The Laugh of the Medusa," we still witness its flashbacks in parliaments, demonstrations, universities or companies, to name just a few places, where women and those assuming "feminine" roles constitute a minority, if not in number then definitely in entitlement and position. The patterns of patriarchal reactions to women—particularly when we bring issues of our exclusion to the public sphere, when we share our suffering and our systematic, if not systemic, nonadmission and limitation in virtually all spheres of life—are hideous. Ridiculing and degrading women, double standards, glass ceilings and sticky floors, uninvited hands roaming our bodies when we are girls, when we are teenagers, when we are adults; at bars, at job interviews, during religion lessons, on buses, at schools and universities; at doctors' offices and dispensaries, in classes and therapies—it happens to us everywhere. Few remember that #MeToo was initiated by African American feminist Tarana Burke back in 2006.[36] It became much more popular in October 2017 when actress Alyssa Milano posted her accusations against Harvey Weinstein on Twitter and 40,000 women responded to her tweet—the #MeToo hashtag was used approximately 12 million times within the first twenty-four hours of her posting it, according to CBS.[37] The #MeToo campaign was led by many highly mediatized court cases, some less visible transitions in the labor sector and a series of further important feminist online campaigns, such as #YesAllWomen or #RapedAndNeverReported. It is difficult to judge the exact repercussions of these campaigns, but some of them were severe, not just for Hollywood producers, but also for other men in corporate leadership roles. The massive response from women online, when we all joined #MeToo and wrote about our experiences of harassment, cannot be ignored—for many of us, not only those identified as women, it was the first time that the horrifying scale of violence against women was really revealed. I believe that the performative efficiency of those millions of hashtags suddenly appearing on online platforms has done more for the general knowledge about violence against women than any earlier action. There are also some very important yet quite invisible implications of #MeToo and similar campaigns—a sense of solidarity and support, all too often ignored within the most popular paradigm of understanding political action as that done by heroes, with heroes and for heroes. In Chapter 4, I argue for a more nuanced understanding of political agency, proposing that the concept of "weak resistance" embraces the crucial yet underestimated aspects of political work like solidarity, endurance or even failure. In the context of #MeToo it is, I believe, essential—yet almost not practiced—to emphasize what it means for people who suffer abuse, sometimes in silence and for decades, to see others sharing similar experiences, supporting each other and expressing solidarity. The importance of such community in struggle is a tricky one to document and measure; however, these difficulties should not legitimize its constant erasure.

I assert that the changes taking place in the art publics, heading toward the emancipation of the public, also apply to the public sphere more generally. The omnipresence of internet media—where not just chosen authors, but what we might call "publics in general" share and comment on messages—is a big step toward a more participatory and emancipated public, *pace* Jodi Dean and others who have understandably criticized the commodification of images and voices that can occur in this context. Our publics emancipate in theaters, media, public debates and television, and this process should also be seen as transversal. It is to some degree mediated by social media and the internet, but this transversality also results from the universalization of higher education, access to information, and so on. While we currently worry, and rightly so, about the expansion of "fake news" and manipulations performed by companies such as Cambridge Analytica, the more emancipated and encouraging side of the picture of the contemporary public cannot be ignored.

All of these issues seem relevant in the current women's protests around the globe. The omnipresence of domestic violence—documented by women's and human rights organizations such as Amnesty International and usually reaching some 30 percent of households, at least in Europe—was a driving force behind the protests held in 2016 and 2017 in Italy, Mexico, Argentina and other countries. Women's protests against the ban on abortion and other severe restrictions were led by Poland, the first country in which we saw massive mobilizations in 2016. These spread to South Korea, Nicaragua, Argentina and Ireland, and in the last of these the protests finally brought an end to the ban in 2018. In the United States, the massive women's protests of 2017 were directed against a particular person, the president, Donald Trump, and his shameless misogyny, announced on different occasions in his public statements. The International Women's Strike, initiated in 2017, gathered women in sixty countries and later became even more global.

The #MeToo campaign has reached much further than expected, gathering women in an array of countries around different kinds of sexual abuse: from the Nobel Academy in Sweden to young leftist journalists in Poland; from heavily mediatized Hollywood scandals to the perhaps less globally visible, yet no less painful, fights against sexual violence and harassment in Bollywood. The campaign allows an unpacking of problems that had been silenced for decades—abuses perpetrated in daylight that nobody seemed to want to see. Now we are all learning different "registers of seeing." We are talking about matters that, until recently, conveniently sat in what Lauren Berlant called "the Oz of America"—the domain of supposedly liberating privacy. By 1999, Berlant had already written about the "normative/ utopian image of the US citizen who remains unmarked, framed, and protected by the private trajectory of his life project, which is sanctified at the juncture where the unconscious meets history: the American Dream."[38] This dream and all the smaller but no less pertinent dreams built in postwar societies (West and East) served to maintain the safety of men in their private lives. In a similar vein, women were—and to some extent, still are—"preserved" from enter- ing the public realm. And language, as it often does without our own invention or intervention, also acts against women in this formula- tion, since a "public woman" still connotes something very different from "public man."

Parallel to social media's global vindication of the public sphere in recent decades and the reassertion of the need for positive body images in the media and for reproductive rights—and given the rise of proudly patriarchal and socially ultraconservative politics—femi- nists today also reclaim cultural archetypes of femininity to dismantle the existing canon. Similarly to Honig's unearthing of Ismene and Antigone's sororal pact, certain artists are now returning to classic female characters to give them new lives. There is only one thing to be done: we must turn the tables of the social staging of the public sphere, undermining its normative, gendered framework.

Honig's theorizing of Antigone as colluding with her sister, Ismene, implies a change in the understanding of women in politics. Instead of favoring women who succeed in the male-dominated politics of today, Honig seems to support these women and forms of activism which go beyond the individualist principle of one actress's heroism and invite alliances, heterogeneity and nonindividualism. Her inter- pretation accentuates acting in common; she argues:

> In her individuality Antigone is, as Hegel would rightly note,
> fated to mere negativity and little more. In their sorority, however,
> the sisters' twinned negotiations of their forced choices model a

> tragically doomed *politics* that is, notwithstanding its tragic character or perhaps even because of that, a more serious force and a more powerful example to feminists now than the individual and sacrificial politics of conscience for which Antigone is traditionally celebrated even by radical feminists.[39]

The critique of liberal individualism is thus taken one step further than in the earlier feminist formulations, where the badly abstract category of "women" was supposed to explain the generalized oppression of one group installed as representative of all.[40] Now we obtain a more specific focus on the heterogeneity of those united in political action. In my opinion, the analysis offered by Honig sublates the philosophy of the many—instead of opting for somehow homogeneous "masses," in which heroic action still wins the biggest applause, we are invited to join forces in tracing specific acts and words that perform resistance via several different people at once acting in unison, for the same cause and in conflicted conditions. If this heterogeneity can be preserved in counterpublics of the common, which I discuss further, it would mean that we move beyond liberalism, finally.

Exclusive liberal norms of the public sphere still govern academia and other sectors of public life, where women have always been designated as unwanted strangers. The expected public subject is, as Carole Pateman and other feminists have argued, shaped to fit masculine socialization and gender roles. The list of "common topics" excludes those attributed to women and femininity, such as bodies, affects and relations. In academia, this means that the conduct of students or professors can be criticized or punished when it expresses anti-discriminatory concerns, but it will be seen as covered by freedom of speech or other constitutional rights and liberties when it is racist, sexist or homophobic. It means that in trying to build a nonsexist academia, we face many more risks than those colleagues who push it toward a discriminatory extreme. Women in academia also face unexpected difficulties when it comes to expectations. If we adapt well in this male-dominated context, we are seen as "resigning from femininity," although some of us—by being butch, intersex, trans, queer or by simply not giving a shit—obviously do not follow this

traditional script in the first place. If we tend to embrace the traditional feminine gender costume, on the other hand, we are seen as
aliens. We risk our every spoken or published word being judged
as somehow determined by our gender, our socialization, or even the
clothes or makeup we might wear. Or we risk being judged by our
affect. For some reason, it seems, from my personal experience,
that people with short hair and trousers are perceived as beings
who do not experience emotions, while those with longer hair and
skirts clearly generate too much affect. Offensive remarks, shouting
or sudden withdrawals are seen as less affective than tears or other
expressions of vulnerability. I won't even bring up the topic of
academics who are also mothers and who, apart from the problems I
have already enumerated, also have to face the risk of being discriminated against in their careers. It is often claimed that after maternity
leave, women are not up to speed on their discipline's newest trends,
or they "do not care" for scholarly developments because of their preoccupation with their children. These nonsensical claims have real
implications for women's lives, making them far less visible among
professors, for example, than men, whose careers proceed "smoothly."

What I just depicted as a woman's experience in academia sounds
very soft in comparison with the very sincere and personal account
offered by Catherine Malabou in her book *Changing Difference*. Her
statement concerns women in philosophy, perhaps the harshest of all
disciplines; however, I believe that some of it resonates also with
women in other parts of academia or in other professions entirely.
She writes: "No doubt women will never become impenetrable, invio-
lable. That's why it is necessary to imagine the possibility of women
starting from the structural impossibility she experiences of not being
violated, in herself and outside, everywhere. An impossibility that
echoes the impossibility of her welcome in philosophy."[41] It is important to note that this comes from a world-renowned philosopher,
famous for her work on Hegel and plasticity.

As feminists in academia, we are often used at our universities as
some kind of extra, unpaid counseling workforce available to handle
every case of masculine misconduct, harassment or discrimination.
From personal experience this rings true, regardless of whether we

are prepared to take up the excess emotional labor since our training is rather in history, microbiology or architecture. In this way, we regularly serve as strong examples of women whose knowledge about gender is used and abused in ways that other scholars never have to deal with. I remember participating in conferences where other people were discussing their presentations, and I was handling cases of discrimination, explaining what gender is and how male privilege was built historically. My papers at these conferences were about Rancière, Althusser, resistance or precarity. Yet it was somehow assumed that I could handle the discussions on my papers or others as well as discussions on every sexist incident that would take place in the conferences. After several drinks in conference receptions later, colleagues mansplained to me that I should always be ready to respond to the needs of any (male) scholar to learn about gender. Additionally, I was told how scary I seem at first, but then how this image changes. I had to prepare useful responses to demands and statements like these—to handle cases of harassment or discrimination, to teach gender studies after hours and so on. This did not prevent one department at Warsaw University from feeling hugely disappointed when, some ten years ago, I refused to work on their antidiscrimination plan for free. Still, some of my colleagues agree to become unpaid equal-status advisors, which makes me wonder: when will we learn that such work should be paid? Over the past few centuries of labor organizing, people have died making sure that workers' rights are respected. What does this painful and admirable past mean if we allow free use of our knowledge and skills to solve problems created in and by patriarchal capitalism? Some of us obviously do it out of good will and necessity, but still: why are we willing to provide unlimited, unpaid extra hours of emotional labor while insisting on negotiating over and being paid for extra hours spent teaching or doing administrative tasks?

This assumption of good will might kill us. I would rather follow the willfulness advised by Sara Ahmed, who has not only theorized the stubborn resistance found in everyday practices of nonconformism, but also resigned from her post at Goldsmiths because the cases of harassment she was tasked with handling as the university's administrative antidiscrimination functionary were going nowhere.[42] As painful as the resignation of a brilliant feminist scholar from a prominent academic position seems, it also delineates certain limits of what can and cannot be tolerated in today's academe. Working in several universities over the last fifteen years, I have seen and experienced the problematic impossibilities, the painful silencing and the rote, violent defensiveness of the academic machine too many times. And there is only one way out: through more feminism and more desire to have it all.

Sara Ahmed published the book *Willful Subjects* in 2014, two years before resigning from her position at Goldsmiths. In this book, she discusses nonheroic models of resistance: obstinacy, error, willfulness, queerness. She argues that "willfulness too has been understood as an error of will . . . This intimacy of willfulness and unhappiness remains to be thought. And to think that intimacy is to queer the will."[43] The book is defined as willful itself, it is also a willful archive, beginning with the Grimm brothers' tale of a "willful child" and following all kinds of philosophical and historical errancy and stubbornness. The "will sphere" and "willing with others" passages in the book add a possible commonality of the willful subject, its potential of being with others and crossing over individualist subjectivity.

The #MeToo campaign is very much about such "willfulness." Questions such as "why do you even talk about this crap?" or "can't you simply let go?" are constantly directed at women and LGBTQ+ persons who reveal the abuse they suffered, often for long years. As inappropriate and nasty as they may be, questions like these also reveal a certain irritation caused by the fact that not everyone accepts the world in which we live. And yet if punching a Nazi is a good sign, why isn't revealing that your boss or professor has been sexually harassing you? What is the difference?

In the precarious neoliberal state of academia, intellectual workers often barely manage to survive. The situation in Eastern Europe is perhaps even more dramatic due to the necessity of "keeping up" with Western academic standards without sufficient means to live. But regardless of academic salaries, which are undergoing substantial cuts worldwide, our work has become an unsustainable combination of administration, teaching, and the production of knowledge. As it stands, the norms of productivity continue to rise at a maddening pace, beyond any logical limits. In his book on the university as a common good, philosopher and researcher Krystian Szadkowski systematically criticizes the neoliberal transformation of the university, clearly demonstrating how knowledge—which requires collective practice, sharing, free access and strategies of support—has become yet another commodity in the capitalist market.[44] This commodification of knowledge does not exempt feminist knowledge, practices or canons, thus transforming our work and its results into fancy products in the marketplace of "creative capital." However, beyond solid Marxist and feminist critique of extant academia, we also need effective resistance to the processes installed through the neoliberal transformation of universities into corporate knowledge industries. As I mentioned, some important work in this area, combining the critique of abuse with resistance, has been done by feminist scholars, among whom Sara Ahmed seems an interesting example from whom to learn. Her strategy was harshly criticized by Angela Davis, who claims that embracing "diversity politics" is a version of assimilation within racist, sexist, corporate academia.[45] While I partially agree with Davis's criticism of diversity politics, I am also much more respectful toward those scholars who have gotten involved in it, shaping (perhaps impossible) patterns of an academia free from discrimination. I would like to stress that while I might have a different vision of how egalitarian academia can be realized, the merit, efforts and often also the price feminist scholars have paid to dismantle sexism and discrimination in academia deserve respect and can be further used in shaping emancipatory practice. Universities are institutions, and institutions, as Mary Douglas very clearly explained in *How Institutions Think*, do not merely structure the surfaces of our beliefs; they shape the deeply rooted core of our existence, including values or beliefs concerning authority and hierarchies.[46] Thus, equality needs to be rehearsed, and what comes with such practice is failure, embracing it and learning to fail better. This observation, usually attributed to Lenin, has its roots in Rosa Luxemburg's correspondence.[47] In this sense, an emancipated academia will unfortunately not jump out of anyone's hat; it can only be built by those who dare to spend time, energy and effort to practice it, most of the time failing, as recent examples have shown, but nevertheless contributing to the general knowledge and practice of equality.[48] An emancipated academia needs to be practiced, sometimes also by failing, otherwise it will remain theory.

I believe that a complaint—in academia and any other workplace— can be effective only if acted against its rules. At the University of Warsaw, where I filed an antidiscrimination complaint, it was only furthered procedurally due to making it a public case. The institution's own system of antidiscriminatory procedures is—as one produced to support the university—ineffective for those complaining. Thus, a counterpublic has to form around the complainant, otherwise it just will not work. In my case, it formed. Some years earlier, at the university in Kraków, students offered the rector an alternative: keeping my job or striking. This proposal was far more effective, though. Assuming—after Douglas and others—that institutions are born to resist change, I can only see an effective complaint as one that involves other actors, rather than just the complainant and the institution; it thus becomes a counterpublic, in which the claim to justice and demand for specific changes become elements of public debate and political action, becoming something else than a complaint. Practiced as an individual claim, kept confidential, the complaint cannot be effective, as Sara Ahmed's work clearly proves. It is important to note that, at least in Poland, the old labor unions either ignore the complainants or, worse, act against them. Such was the case of the ZNP union in Kraków, which, instead of informing me of my rights, or supporting me, as I'd requested, threatened me and tried to force my agreement with the dean, who accused me of an impossible crime. The union's representative later apologized; however, being threatened by a supposedly left-leaning union in a moment of struggle and incredible accusations is something I still feel some pain about, although many years have passed. In Warsaw, the new union, syndicalist in profile, Inicjatywa Pracownicza (the Worker's Initiative; a union following the IWW model and political profile), fully supported my case, together with students and some faculty. The ZNP remained silent. And the university's Solidarność representatives went to a dean of the department where I had studied fifteen years ago but had never worked—a dean known for his negative opinion of me, formed mainly virtually, as we almost never met—and asked his perspective, which obviously was very critical, and they shared it with me. For someone whose father spent months in jail to defend Solidarność back in the 1980s, that was a painful experience as well.

As we can discern from this short study of feminist lives within academia, feminist counterpublics need it all—we need to work transversally across the different formats and groups. Clearly one-person victories are not sufficient at all, and in academia—shaped to meet the individualist model—forming groups is not easy. However, it does happen, and it can happen on a larger scale as well. Unions, journalists, engaged faculty members and students, lawyers and feminists—all those persons and groups can form feminist counterpublics in academia and, similarly, in other workplaces.

Some years ago, Nancy Fraser warned about feminism becoming a willing "handmaiden" to capitalism.[49] She rightly criticized the assimilationist trends in feminism, particularly its readiness to accept basic capitalist elements, such as inequality, outsourcing, deregulation and so on. I believe Fraser's warnings were perhaps too general; there are feminist scholars, initiatives and groups fiercely resisting neoliberal marketization. However, her critique remains a necessary alarm in times of accelerated capitalist appropriation. Fraser's harsh critique of feminist assimilation into the market economy strongly resonates in Poland. Her warning gave a sense of purpose to left-leaning feminists—who have always constituted a minority—and instilled a certain fear in our mainstream liberal counterparts. Since the early 1990s, the latter group has demonstrated a much greater willingness to embrace capitalist logic, using, for example, the supposedly repressive postwar state communism as an excuse for their lack of interest in opposing class exclusions, discrimination and violence in their versions of feminism. This reality has been particularly harsh in countries where the International Monetary Fund and World Bank have dictated every aspect of the transition to neoliberal capitalism.

An uncritical embrace of the market economy has made it almost impossible to defend women's rights against the market. Through precarization, privatization and other aspects of the transformation, women became victims of state withdrawal, including losing social security benefits that they enjoyed before 1989. At the same time, women took up the responsibilities of care no longer provided by employers and the state. Sudden rashes of unemployment, reductions in public services, and general insecurity resulted in a greater demand for care and affective labor from women. We became the support networks for all those rejected by a changing system.[50] This burden, combined with precarization and the sudden introduction of Poland's antiabortion law in 1993 and restricted access to reproductive services more generally, made women the primary victims of the country's neoliberal capitalism.[51] In such a situation, one would expect mainstream feminism to be at least socialist. But no: liberation from the supposed oppressive regime of the People's Republic of Poland has petrified the feminist political imagination for decades. And as Briony Lipton rightly argues, "neoliberalism appears resistant to nuanced criticism precisely because it has individualised and internalised the norms of capitalist logic and self-interest (Skeggs), making it difficult to articulate these new forms of inequality."[52] This should be another reason for searching neoliberalism's feminist critique, otherwise gender inequalities, as well as the oppression and discrimination of LGBTQ+ persons, will once again be made invisible by critics, who assume that feminism only happens on television.

The women's movement, in Poland and globally, acts as a multitude of feminist counterpublics for the defense of women's rights through its insistence on overturning the division between public and private, in its emphasis on women's oppression and in its twofold resistance to the conservative powers of the government and the neoliberal powers within the existing public sphere. The dissent and the transversal feminist movement that formed around the protests of 2016 immediately challenged other elements of right-wing politics in Poland. These issues included the ecological disaster in the old-growth forest of Białowieża, air pollution, court reforms (which have subordinated the courts to the state's executive power), fascist demonstrations, and breaches of labor rights, among many other matters. Women also joined forces across borders—through the International Women's Strike and beyond—and online campaigns like #MeToo were fundamental to this work. We are still counting the repercussions of these sudden connections.

Today, almost every panel at a public event or otherwise in which women are not contributing is immediately criticized. So too are the public statements of politicians who sexualize or otherwise discriminate against women. This is a big change. Even as recently as 2015, these kinds of practices went unnoticed and were seen as "normal." The Black Protests and Women's Strike transformed public debate in Poland, drawing more attention to the #MeToo actions that came later. They also gained strength and international connections after these campaigns. Several journalists and politicians were accused by their partners and/or co-workers of sexual harassment, abuse or rape. Young feminist journalists publicly revealed the names of two young leftist journalists who had sexually assaulted them. The accusers and their supporters are now fighting backlash from liberal circles, but their actions also helped to reshape the standards of gender relations in Poland.

It is difficult to enumerate all the different groups and feminist visions animating such a global movement. One thing is certain, however: the logic of solidarity and internationalism has begun to replace a narrow liberal agenda, transforming the narrative of "choice" (as if women in Poland, Argentina or Nicaragua had a choice) into one of collective resistance, critique of patriarchal capitalism and a rejection of compromise.[53] Due to the universality of the demands of today's women-led protests—which focus on such far-reaching topics such as abortion, the misogynist policies of Trump and other right-wing political leaders, and violence against women—feminist movements worldwide are transforming. They are becoming more *common* and less elitist, more popular and less exclusive. The meaning of "the common" is shifting from a preoccupation with what is shared and collective to a concern for the ordinary, the mundane, the everyday; in broadening its meaning in this way, the common gains strength.[54] With this shift, the utopian dimension of the common is expanded to embrace a more heterotopic sense of what can be done.

The feminist counterpublics created in the women's protests of 2016–17 and fueled by #MeToo and other campaigns, as well as the mass declarations of women who took part in these actions, still constitute hope for a revival of progressive politics in Poland as well as globally. In the state of exception created by the PiS government and strengthened every day by the further privileging of executive powers and massive scandals concerning every domain of life, women acted as those who have only their chains to lose—and we won without reviving the heroic myths of resistance. In the emphasis on the weakness of our condition, threatened by the antiabortion bill but also by the "gender wars" reducing us to reproductive functions, we used the ordinary, common strategies of basic solidarity and resistance—and this, not any heroic figures or bravery, made a successful movement possible.

3

Counterpublics of the Common in Communication Capitalism

Counterpublics and institutions of the common present themselves as strikingly similar on the level of social practice, as well as in their theoretical composition. However—as I did not discuss this problem systematically—their proximity, similarities and the prospects of combining them are all analyzed here. Communication capitalism is a notion proposed by Jodi Dean to dismantle the ideological stakes hidden behind supposed "free debate" in the internet, which many take to be the contemporary public sphere. This notion proves particularly helpful in depicting new media today; however, I also point to certain limitations of the perspective that are rooted in the supposedly overwhelmingly general notion of ideology and argue for embracing exceptions in the ideological reproduction of communication capitalism.

Antonio Negri and Michael Hardt's book series—opening with *Empire* and following with *Multitude*, *Commonwealth* and *Assembly*—provided a complex and highly praised conceptual framework for understanding the common. As well, the notion of "institutions of the common," as it appears in the work of Gerald Raunig, proposes an interesting combination of critical praxis and affective organization of the resisting social realm. His perspective moves between certain elements of critical theory with Spinozean "non-individualism." As for counterpublics, I will mainly focus on Kluge and Negt's theory. It needs to be stressed that this chapter is not a discussion of these authors' entire philosophical projects; I will focus only on specific parts of their work, highlighting it and sometimes proposing interpretations, which might seem to go against the authors' intentions. I believe, however, that without such readings theory simply becomes a monumental archive.

In Hardt and Negri's *Commonwealth*, the common is presented as an alternative to the public/private, as a version of a "third way," particularly in the context of property, which is neither individualized nor institutionalized by the state, but shared by everyone or at least groups of people. As they emphasize, humanity is not separated from the environment, it is a part of it, constantly interactive, as in breathing (the air is one example of a commons), walking (the landscape is a commons), doing art (culture is a form of a commons), speaking (yes, languages are commons too, this is a great example, actually) and so on.[1] The common is very clearly lived and experienced, shared, not owned, and built in production, not just bought, although the extent of the corruption of the common by market exchanges, colonization and other capitalist processes is obviously contested throughout the book. This aspect of the common as shared, lived and materialized experience involving human and nonhuman agents, makes it similar to the lived experience of counterpublics, as depicted in Kluge and Negt, as well as Fraser. However, in their formulations, human agency is always central, while I believe the project of Negri and Hardt is far more sympathetic toward embracing nonhuman agency, following the cyberfeminism and transhumanism of Donna Haraway, who is one of the important references in their books. In Kluge and Negt's *Public Sphere and Experience*, counterpublics are presented as the political agency of those involved in production, with their needs and demands not divided into those "particular" and "general," as happens in liberal political models, such as the one offered by Habermas. Specifically, economy is not separated from politics, as in many liberal political projects, and it constitutes a vital context of political claims making, which is the core of counterpublics. The counterpublics of proletarians, however, involve industrial production landscapes and machines, thus opening the possibility of envisioning humans as participating in the material world rather than being separate from it; likewise in moments of political decision making. Let's imagine the Gdańsk shipyard; the strike and its impact on various aspects of social life in Poland were made possible by the engagement of humans in a specific, strategically crucial territory—one inhabited by the huge iron cranes, the ships and their parts, the vast spaces of land and water, and also tramways, particularly the one eventually stopped by Henryka Krzywonos in the city center, thus spreading information about the strike, as I wrote earlier. The machines do not participate in liberal political decision making. Most of humanity also does not, because of the class, gender and ethnic inequality, which—explicitly, as in Aristotle, or implicitly, in modern liberal political projects—allows for the separation (of the "personal" and the "political," the "particular" and the "common") vital for the classic public sphere, while in counterpublics, as well as for the common—it is either contradicted or sublated.

In *Assembly*, Negri and Hardt write: "We must . . . challenge the process of emptying the public and the capitalist right to extract and privatize the common, but also demistify and combat the neoliberal process of subjection."[2] They emphasize the ways in which neoliberalism became a politics of liquidating the public sector into private property, by explicit transitions of state ownership status or by more implicit moves, such as diminishing collective power over institutions, land and other forms of the public. What was public melts into the private, one could say, paraphrasing Marshall Berman. Also, a reference to Zygmunt Bauman's concepts of "liquid modernity" and "liquid love" is relevant here, as neoliberal biopolitics restructures stable institutions and affects into their distant, precarious shadows. As labor is central in Hardt and Negri's ontology, resistance to neoliberal politics obviously should be expected, and I believe that I will not misinterpret their work by arguing that the concept of the general strike, which they generously discuss in *Assembly*, reminds one of the proletarian public sphere, being at once a site of oppositional demands rooted in production and the form of organizing beyond neoliberal governmentality.[3] The reference to a general strike might only seem nostalgic (although isn't it?). However, here in Poland, and I try to emphasize this in Chapter 2 as well as now, we had an experience of an actual general strike in 1980, which is how Solidarność was born.

It was a great surprise to see the beginning of this movement listed alongside the Zapatistas and alterglobalization, because this is what it was—a common in revolt, opposing the repressive and bureaucratic aspects of the ruling Workers' Party of Poland, not socialism as a political system, as I emphasized earlier.[4] This experience of an effective general strike confirms the intuitions expressed by Hardt and Negri concerning the possibilities of institutionalizing the common, with all the risks and limitations such a project involves. The strike—after the agreements of August 1980—transformed into a registered union, with 10 million registered members, some of them combining this with Communist Party membership, and a system of councils organizing both unions and public institutions.

Hardt and Negri rightly ask whether reform is impossible.[5] Their answer, however, is a critical one, as they move the focus from the possibility to the conditions of possibility, just as Immanuel Kant did in his refreshing take on the possibility of cognition in *Critique of Pure Reason*. Hardt and Negri therefore ask about the origins and content of our definitions of reform and revolution, and they—again, rightly—demand a revision of those two notions, which have organized the progressive, radical, leftist imagination for centuries. They assume that our images of reform and revolution were born in industrial capitalism, mainly in Europe, and thus they cannot organize a globalized revolution two centuries later. I believe this observation is absolutely crucial—the politics of contemporary counterpublics, be it of the common or otherwise, cannot be prisoner to the visions of strategy and tactics so dated—and thus so very inaccurate. In *Commonwealth*, they discuss Caliban, a figure they take from Shakespeare, but also built in the discussion of early modernity offered by Silvia Federici and other authors. The reference to a colonized, Black, enslaved rebel leads to the necessity of embracing the historical rebellions led by non-Europeans against Europeans, but not against such central European modern values as equality. The work of Susan Buck-Morss on Hegel and Haiti shows the extent to which Europe is actually indebted to the radical politics of the colonized. The work of Achille Mbembe demands a recognition of the Black cultural and intellectual traditions ignored and destroyed by the colonial superpowers. These works show, I believe, that the vulnerable tissue of our political imagination can be interwoven between futures—as Hardt and Negri, the accelerationists, cyberfeminists and xenofeminists show—but also between forgotten, foreclosed and repressed pasts.

Within the lines of Hardt and Negri's discussion of revolution, reform and the strike, another concept appears—that of "counterpowers," which bears some resemblance to counterpublics. The counterpowers are described as those that need to remain in antagonistic relation, subverting capitalist sovereignty.[6] Counterpowers are central for constituting the "new Prince," who can appear after they "(1) attack the vertical axis and empty its repressive power and (2) construct against it counterpowers formed in the horizontal axis of social production and reproduction; (3) only then, when the construction of counterpowers is achieved, can a new Prince initiate a process of constituent power."[7] Before discussing this proposition, which needs to be critically addressed, partially on the grounds of the very project of the new Prince as Negri and Hardt build it, I would like to quote another fragment from *Assembly* that elucidates their political project in a much clearer and uncontroversial way. Discussing the problem of leadership, Negri and Hardt write:

> Against alienated (that is, isolated, individualized, instrumentalized) labor arises a common resistance, which in the industrial regime was expressed most powerfully as a refusal of work and today is expressed in the new forms of antagonism that are active across the entire social terrain. Constituent power can thus no longer be conceived in purely political terms and must be mixed with social behaviors and new technologies of subsistence, resistance, and transformation of life. The process of the construction of new institutions must be absorbed into this new materiality.[8]

As mentioned in various critical discussions of Negri and Hardt's theory of the Empire, there is a contradiction between the highly idealist distinction between the (oppressive) now and the (emancipated) project, on the one hand, and a very materialist, brilliant understanding of the materiality of current modes of capitalist production, their antagonisms and the process of politicizing the multitude transversally, across the established borders and distinctions, on the other. Jodi Dean emphasizes a similar contradiction in her analysis of Hardt and Negri's take on communication, where she praises their description of what she calls "communication capitalism," yet she finds the alternatives to it impossible in the versions these authors formulate.[9] As we will see in the discussion of media and politics, this controversy is an inspiring yet quite fundamental one, for some making it impossible to ally with their project, for others demanding a solution and thus adding to the development of radical politics. As clearly stems from what I have written up to now, I am a rather excited representative of the second option.

In their critiques of the capitalist mode of production, Negri and Hardt emphasize the artificiality and segregation of various aspects of life. At the very core of the notion of the common lies the premise of a reunion of life, undivided between private and public ownership; in the discussions of organizing labor according to the principles of solidarity and collaboration lies a premise of voluntary organization, reminiscent of Abramowski's or Kropotkin's collaborative anarchism, Foucauldian concept of biopolitics as one of the solutions to the Cartesian division of body and soul and Hegel's divides inherent in the dialectics built on oppositions. And then we read that the new Prince can only initiate their constituent power after counterpowers are installed. This clear division between the before and after obviously opposes the otherwise transversal images of the multitude becoming the common. Such sharp division can only be projected apart from politics being produced within heterogeneous, emergent and contradictory social movements, whose spontaneity seems to be respected by Negri and Hardt in their other texts. This contradiction in the context of media has a similar form: neoliberal governmentality spreads throughout immaterial labor, especially in cultural production, and yet somehow the multitude manages to oppose it. The very concept of immaterial labor, still central in *Empire* and the next volume, *Multitude,* was criticized, particularly by feminist theorists, as inaccurate in how it erases the materialized processes of production and reproduction. This contradiction, however, was quite swiftly resolved by the transition from "immaterial labor" to "biopolitical labor," explained most fully in *Commonwealth*, and I believe it is a good trajectory.

I believe that Félix Guattari and his concept of transversality may help in rethinking the depicted contradiction without erasing its powerful theoretical stakes. *The Three Ecologies* offers a radical strategy for transition and social change that cuts across the borders of institution-noninstitution, public-private, social-political, individual-collective and so on.[10] It might sound superficially optimistic; however, this notion allows an understanding of feminism's "march through institutions" and through social strata, cultural differences and forms of agency, as well as legal systems. Transversality is a notion aimed at avoiding the binary oppositions and the heritage of dialectics, allowing political theory to move forward and embrace heterogeneity without necessarily resigning its radical aims. It stretches the understanding of new ideas as those that move in different directions, and may—as feminism did—penetrate all of the social realm. It also provides a nonessentializing, ethical position. It likewise mediates the supposedly impossible passage from capitalist reality, corrupt and oppressive, toward emancipated futures. Radical affects, so praised in *Empire* but also in *Public Sphere and Experience,* form in the conditions of oppression, whether such oppression is fought in grassroots communities or state institutions. I will return to this problem later.

The common of Negri and Hardt's work meets Kluge and Negt's proletarian counterpublics in recognizing the central position of the subject formation for contemporary capitalism, although they wrote in the 2010s and 1970s, respectively. This recognition of the fundamental meaning of the "lived experience," as Kluge and Negt put it, or the "production of subjects," as Negri and Hardt say it, and the strategy of locating it at the core of the contemporary process of production situates these two distanced theoretical approaches to the public in sharp opposition to liberal political doctrine and in close proximity to one another. In *Public Sphere and Experience,* the ideological totality of the bourgeois experience has to be contradicted by the lived experience of those involved in production, because it is there—and not in the bad abstraction of the liberal public sphere, that the genuine public is produced. In both approaches, the public shall not be merely a decontextualized, disembodied sphere of (badly) abstracted common and debate. Both ways lead to an expression of political needs rooted in the experience of production—of the subjects and of the common more generally. Still, while the proletarian counterpublics lack the affective impulses to allow resistance, the common acts as if it "could not speak" (in a sense given to Gayatri Spivak's formulation—as if the capitalist logics of ideological reproduction did not allow such speech acts).[11] Only combining the affective, embodied multitude with a clearly critical focus allows for dismantling the neoliberal double bind, in which creativity is always already profitable, corrupting radical impulses before they even appear.

The production of subjectivity, as discussed in *Assembly,* might at first seem a repetition of liberal individualist ontology. Yet it is not, as processes of production, resistance and building solidarity always seem to be lived by the many, not by one—therefore they are plural and interconnected. The multitude—Spinoza's concept and the perspective Negri and Hardt take on the human part of the social— resembles the people under construction, a not yet divided or fully formed mass, one easily feared, as Warren Montag shows, or reduced to "rabble," as was depicted by Frank Ruda, or excluded as the historical losers, in Walter Benjamin's "barbarians."[12] The transition of the rebellious multitude in the common differs from the origins of society presented in classical modern theory, where it is by means of property distribution (Locke), cultural organization (Rousseau) or the desire to accomplish chosen aims (Kant) that the social is created. In Spinoza, and after him, in Hardt and Negri, the social forms itself following structures of affect, which work across individualist logic. This is a key difference of their model from the other conceptualizations of the social, where the principle of individuation is projected on every part of society. Such affective structure of social organization is perhaps the most peculiar to study, as it does not provide a clear grid of social relations (as in Locke and Hume), nor does it champion the primacy of rational choices, as in Kant. It is the least predictable yet perhaps most accurate depiction of the social. Hegelian dialectics cut across such distinctions, providing a model of the social, in which all of the aforementioned aspects are synthetically combined as history, unfolding in its insecure and yet quite predictable way. As Žižek correctly pointed out, Hegel's thought was long a captive of the flattened rationalism, reductive idealism and various ideologies of history. Meanwhile, his ability to capture the affective and subconscious structures of human development, recently rediscovered by the Slovenian School, allows a new multilayered theory of the social, where its drives and ironies play a historical and not solely descriptive role.

The multitude and its transition into the common has one other important aspect, constituted by embracing the commons—air, languages, landscapes, "resources" and so on—a constitution perhaps best suited for the thinking shaped in the context of the anthropocene, yet by emphasizing the social dimension, it does not flatly resign from the political. This is an aspect of Negri and Hardt's theory perhaps most ignored and, on the other hand, also most inspiring for thinking through political theory in times of global ecological catastrophe. Such commons—organized by the affective structures of the multitude—can develop in a fascist or progressive direction. In order to avoid the darkest option—a strong, critical position has to be embraced, however—and not an idealist one (and by idealist, I mean theories detached from the experience of the social) but one embracing the diversity of social production. In this aspect, the combination of commons and counterpublics seems perhaps most hopeful in targeting ideological reproduction not by means of smashing the remnants of resisting countercultures and institutions, but by way of reconfiguring the political imagination together in struggle.

Gerald Raunig's claims to overcome individualism were articulated in his theory of dividuum, as well as on the level of social ontology, particularly when he embraces the model of occupation as one allowing a version of instituting the common.[13] In *Dividuum*, he argues that "whereas the concept of individuality tends toward constructing closure, dividual singularity emphasizes similarity in diverse single things, and thus also the potentiality of connecting, appending, concantenating."[14] The ontology of such singularity is deduced from Epicurean and medieval ontologies, in which the process of subject formation is taken to the molecular level, and there such aspects as relations and connections are emphasized to a far greater extent than in the modern ontologies, with the exception of Spinoza. His model of occupation embraces the possibility of taking over state-run institutions that have the status of "public," such as museums, opera houses, schools or universities. It assumes the possibility of transitioning a state institution to an institution of the common, under several conditions: inventing "new instituent practices," reterritorializing and molecularizing existing institutions. A vision of an institution that focuses solely on keeping some art collections (education, music, and so on) and sharing them with the wider public is not one of the common; one that embraces constant transitions is. Sympathizing with his vision of such insurgent instituent practice, I only have one doubt: does the common really need to be so inventive? Is it not one of the central commandments of neoliberal productivity, also criticized by Raunig in his book *Factories of Knowledge, Industries of Creativity,* to reinvent oneself all the time? Is this not the most commodified mode of existence? And, thus, could the common resign from self-reinventing just for the sake of refusing, or even escaping, the high-efficiency norms imposed by neoliberal capitalism?

In the search for institutions to occupy and, further, to practice the transition toward institutions of the common, I always imagine very traditional institutions, such as universities or opera houses, to be the starting point. It is then easy to imagine how some parts of such a project would constantly evolve, but some—decided upon through a collective process, obviously—would stay intact. I imagine the prospect of reading Hegel not just for one semester—which I could only do due to the constant demand for innovation—but for twenty consecutive years without reinventing myself. It sounds so very liberating! (Please do check my bio to see the list of institutions and projects with which I have been involved in the last twenty years). In Central Europe, we have some highly democratic institutions that still function like the councils of inhabitants of houses. This mode of collective decision making is highly democratic, with all the pros and cons, and I do not think this should be abolished solely because the state ordered it in early 1950s. We have parks, museums, galleries, opera houses and theaters that function in democratic ways, sometimes to an extent hard to imagine even in grassroots groups. The essentialist rejection of these institutions sounds terrifying, especially in Warsaw, where we already had our city ruined (75 percent of its buildings were destroyed by the Nazis in WWII). Imagining the effort to destroy and rebuild large sectors of the social realm sounds positively annoying, and thus Raunig's praise for occupation and new instituent powers seems so very promising.

Raunig is quite clear as to where he posits himself in the debate concerning "what is to be done." He says, very accurately: "We can neither go on fetishizing practice and activism as territories beyond theory production (as some protagonists of artivism seem to have it), nor go on privileging the cynical rule of negativity, shying away from getting our hands dirty (as certain anti-activist strands of contemporary theory do."[15] I appreciate his position on this, and I have seen him in places seldom visited by intellectuals, such as borders, deportation centers and prisons. It is quite similar to the stance taken by Negri—a constant partisan for sometimes lost causes, a public intellectual not by means of state or corporate sponsorship, but by genuine involvement in the common. This tradition and sense of participation is almost absent in today's academic and intellectual circles, where the position of splendid isolation became a part of the spectacular doctrine of "public" intellectuals.

In *Assembly,* Negri and Hardt argue for the "counterpowers" that would be horizontal, merged in social production and reproduction. These would lead to the creation of new constituent power. They discuss three strategies, which should be seen and practiced and are complementary: the strategies of exodus, "antagonistic reformism" and the overcoming of existing institutions by creating new ones.[16] Their counterpowers assume the same functions as counterpublics: they are there to resist, transform, oppose, criticize and unite the opposition. Their difference consists merely in the emphasis on communication/articulation in counterpublics and being/acting together in counterpowers, yet, if analyzed closely, these functions are the same—the principle of solidarity constitutes both. An articulation of demands has to happen in a sense of affective community, and the community needs communication. Thus, I assume that the counterpowers of Negri and Hardt and the counterpublics of Kluge and Negt are actually very similar, although they were conceptualized in different philosophical traditions.

I would like to argue that this similarity allows for proposing such political entities as counterpublics of the common. In their opposition to existing forms of the political, in their overcoming of the distinction between reformism and revolutionary strategies, in their ways of transforming existing institutions and in their negation of the unequal class structure, they fulfill the basic functions of counterpublics, allowing for the inclusion of reproductive labor and the formation of subjectivities. This is how the two distinct traditions of critical and operaist Marxism meet, years after the first expressions of these two different currents.

In a conference I asked Toni Negri whether "the multitude can speak," following the critical intention expressed in Gayatri Spivak's famous essay *Can the Subaltern Speak?* Toni said that yes, obviously it can. However, can it also speak as the common? Thus, can it produce a claim (or a set of demands)? I believe the ontology of immanence does not make this task easier. In the Hegelian/Marxist logic organizing the work and ontology of Kluge and Negt, the claim of proletarian counterpublics is one embedded in the context of production, expressing their demands and desires (yes, theirs is an affective Marxism as well; they directly reference Wilhelm Reich) but also overcoming the political ideology of the bourgeoisie, which organizes any political experience as one rooted in the experience of the upper classes.[17] The multitude, on the other hand, while it organizes as the common, clearly overcomes biopolitical neoliberal governance, thus also—although by transformation rather than opposition—overcoming bourgeois hegemony. The differences between the discussed approaches—that of Negri and Hardt and that of Kluge and Negt—should not be overlooked; however, as they emphasize two distinct elements of contemporary politics—exclusivism and conformity—

only together can they fully express the sense of disappropriation of the masses in today's politics. I believe that the ability of the multitude to speak actually requires a critical perspective on the muting powers of the political ideologies of liberal conservatism (yes, I do think that every liberalism has its conservative elements, and most conservatisms embrace liberal elements, like democracy as the political organization of the state). In their claims concerning the audacity of "speaking the truth" and courage, as depicted in the beginning of *Commonwealth*, they clearly embrace critical intention, as well as Kant—who is suddenly praised by theorists who would never do it if not absolutely necessary. This necessity of critique constitutes a natural opposition to neoliberal biopolitics. But it is not only "historically necessary," as Hegelians might argue. First and foremost, the collective claim is a fundamental element of genuine politics, one that does not follow the post-, meta- or pseudo-political evasion of conflict.[18] As I already signaled, thinkers as diverse as Ranciére, Žižek and Mouffe accuse neoliberal politics of actually avoiding the political, which they understand as conflict. Habermas—whom they all rightly criticize for his idealist vision of communication as not only possible (which already is a complicated position) but also as present in contemporary politics (this is already an overstatement) and accessible for everyone (this is pure ideology)—got one thing right: communication understood as collective action is perhaps not the essence of politics, but it definitely constitutes the essence of oppositional politics. If we look at Solidarność, at alterglobalization, the feminist movements or any other counterpublics, what do we see? People communicating and discovering not only the possibility of communication, but also a sense of solidarity and community built within such situations. Obviously, being together in the streets, as Warren Montag and Judith Butler argue, in their very different ways, is the form of public sphere in which discourse is a secondary factor, because what matters above all is the bodies being connected in space. But this connection of bodies exists also in flash mobs, armies and shopping centers, so what makes a demonstration different? A common claim, right? Thus, establishing a way of expressing this factor, among other factors organizing the "bodies in protest" (Butler's formula), becomes crucial even for theories of politics that overcome, and rightly so, rationalist ontology and its political ideologies, such as Habermas's theory of the public sphere.

Theories of counterpublics, on the other hand, fully capable of building the critical analysis of oppositional collectivities gathering around common claims, tend to restrict their ontology to discursive practices and debate, as can be seen in the theory of feminist counter publics of Nancy Fraser, where not much more is left in politics than speaking (bodies, yes). Thus—the proposition of a counterpublics of the common allows imagining a solution, which seems inevitable, a combination of critical theory and Spinozean biopolitics.

In Paul Preciado's amazing book *Testo Junkie*, he argues that perhaps the multitude is today part of the commodified pharma-pornographic market. "The goal of contemporary critical theory would be to unravel our condition as pharmacopornographic workers/consumers. If the current theory of the feminization of labor omits the cum shot, conceals videographic ejaculation behind the screen of cooperative communication, it's because, unlike Houellebecq, the philosophers of biopolitics prefer not to reveal their position as customers of the global pharmacopornomarket."[19] Questions such as "Can the multitude have sex? What are its sexual organs?" thus seem inevitable, contradicting the rather optimistic and unspecified visions of good bodies versus bad institutions so common among defenders of Negri, Hardt or even Butler—although such tendencies cannot, I believe, be found in their texts. However, the issue of sexual expression—and its practice, discourse and commodification and the alternatives to it—is fundamental in any critical social theory and politics. Also, sexuality, as the territory of desire and the subconscious, is often separated as nonpolitical or irrational. However, while only marginally in both theories of counterpublics and the common, it is always present and, in the Fordist capitalist and biopolitically neoliberal forms of political organization of the social, it occupies a key position as a sphere easily disciplined but having implications for a large spectrum of phenomena, allowing the organization of society and introducing various degrees and formats of governmentality throughout the social realm.

Kluge and Negt's book has rightly been criticized for its lack of acknowledgement of gender differences and reproductive labor. Both authors acknowledged this criticism in their later book, *History and Obstinacy*, where they also made some effort to embrace housework and reproductive and affective labor in their analysis of capitalist society. [20] Interestingly, in their critical recapitulation of the history of capitalism and various forms of obstinacy and resistance against it, they follow a somewhat "rhizomatic" method, in many ways similar to that applied by Deleuze and Guattari in *A Thousand Plateaus*. Although an in-depth analysis of these two inspiring books, both published around 1980, is not possible here, I would like to emphasize how the two supposedly contradicting paradigms, the critical and the post-Spinozean, seem to approach each other in an effort to propose a materialist theory embracing experience and affect. In *A Thousand Plateaus*, the politics of desire is depicted as one organized in the structures built and dismantled by drives, while in *History and Obstinacy* it is the constitution and organization of labor that orchestrates the ontology of the social. In both books, images have an important role, working similarly to how Hegel depicted "examples"— as efforts to undermine and contradict the thesis rather than as a stabilizing summary.[21] In his films, Kluge has embraced reproductive labor at least since the 1970s, depicting abortion and housework as fundamental social phenomena as he tried to film Marx's *Capital*.

Both of Kluge and Negt's books, which I discuss here, strongly emphasize the role of media. In *Public Sphere and Experience*, their perspective is still very embedded in the rather pessimistic, one-sided position developed by Adorno and Horkheimer in their *Dialectic of Enlightenment*, where, in the chapter on "cultural industries," today seen as classic, they built an image of the media as capitalism's main system of ideological reproduction.[22] This perspective, practically repeated by Habermas in the chapters on media in *The Structural Transformation of the Public Sphere* from 1962, still resonates in *Public Sphere and Experience*, making it almost impossible to imagine any form of emancipation of the proletariat. Likewise, Negri and Hardt, in their *Empire* and later, have worked toward an ontology of new media, which somehow naturally became an object worthy of critique from Jodi Dean and other Marxist thinkers, as well as toward a theory of resistance, which—if understood as happening on various levels of the biopolitical struggle, also embraces the media. I believe some parts of counterpowers can be seen as media-oriented, and the internet and independent media are expressions of the common, in struggle with private ownership on the one hand and state governance on the other. Before I enter the sometimes heated debates concerning the media and politics in the context of counterpublics of the common, I would like to briefly sketch some earlier polemics concerning the media, so that the current struggles and debates are contextualized.

The seductive and manipulative powers of the media, somewhat demonized in the classic works of the main representatives of the Frankfurt School, have since been contradicted by Marshall McLuhan in his powerful yet perhaps not analytically sustainable works focusing on the transitive aspects of new technologies. In McLuhan's work, "the medium is the message" and thus the analysis of agency within the social ontology focused on the media has to embrace not only the implications of this format but also the transformative power of technologies of communication on the very message, including its content and the intentions behind it.[23] An alternative to critical theory's one-dimensional vision of the media, which is far more relevant for the analysis of counterpublics and the common developed here, is obviously that which came from the radical cultural studies of Stuart Hall and other scholars. In emphasizing the role of audiences of media messages and studying their receptive mechanisms, Hall undermines the merely passive image of media spectatorship, arguing for a theory of media that embraces a plethora of possible reactions to media messaging rather than a monolithic vision of its reception. In the essay "Encoding, Decoding," Hall undermines the very foundations of the classical ontology of media, which is dominated by a sense of separation of its various elements.[24] According to Hall, the message, sender, receiver and other elements of media work are not separated entities; they interact, but more importantly, this interaction has its own dynamics and diversity that is invisible in the stabilizing perspective of classical media theory. In the context of television, information is not only formatted in a way suitable for broadcasting, but it also has to be received in an intended way: "It must first be appropriated as a meaningful discourse and be meaningfully decoded."[25] Hall depicts a spectrum of possible conflicts, contradictions, misunderstandings or merely mistakes, which can appear on the level of formulating and receiving the communication.[26] A similar critique of the solely passive reception of media and art can be found in Jacques Rancière's analysis of the publics and failures of critical art in *The Emancipated Spectator*.[27] Today's audiences and participants of art projects are often as educated as the artists, and their cultural competence should not be neglected in didactic efforts to guide them to a better world. Such guidance is actually experienced as demagogy, and many art projects intended as political simply fail due to the inability to assume a participatory rather than vertical model of communication.

Participants of contemporary counterpublics can be seen as well prepared for using media politically; however, critical theory often still dissimulates this ability of the public. In her review of Habermas's *Structural Transformation of the Public Sphere*, Dana Polan notices that "Habermas presents culture as a type of media and so offers no analysis precisely of why cultural spectacles (like 'Oprah') grip us." She adds: "But all too often the linguistic substitution of one for the other brings with it a semantic shift in thinking of culture as media we lose some of the things we might take culture to be about."[28] Polan contradicts the old, conservative notions of culture as a special, elitist sphere, and she rightly contests Habermas's tendency to praise the bourgeois, supposedly more critically inclined viewer over proletarians, who are perceived as unprepared to critically receive media content. As the studies of Hall—and more recent texts by Halberstam— have shown, neither level of education nor cultural capital secure the appearance of resistance, failure or other disturbances in the distribution and reception of the media message. Sometimes it is by sheer mistake, or sometimes such phenomena as "glitches," misunderstandings or mistakes, torpedo the fluency of ideological reproduction.

In his review of Kluge and Negt's *Public Sphere and Experience*, Fredric Jameson offers a similar critique to Polan's. He argues that while the promise Kluge and Negt make—to provide an alternative to Habermas's conservative theory of the public sphere—seems particularly interesting, and their critique is outstanding, they do not depart from the biased perspective of the workers as less educated than the bourgeoisie and thus as incapable of resisting media's spreading of dominant ideology.[29] They do, however—and this makes them strikingly similar to Negri and Hardt—focus on labor and experience, thus evading the logic of separation and joining Raymond Williams and other nonstructuralist thinkers. It should be emphasized, however, that—as Jameson rightly points out—the language of the proletarian public sphere does not exist.[30] The supposed non-existence of this proletarian public realm explains such lack, as well as historical and political exclusions, foreclosures and domination of the proletariat. Here I need to disagree with Jameson, though—proletarian counterpublics do exist. And they speak, however—as Spivak demonstrated in a different context—the impossibility of such speech to be formulated and received constitutes a fundamental condition of the western Subject.

In her essay "Why the Net is Not a Public Sphere," Jodi Dean makes an important argument concerning the popular belief that depicts the internet as a new public sphere.[31] With clarity and precision, she dismantles the hopes organizing the (mainly liberal) belief in the supposedly egalitarian, inclusive and thus emancipatory character of online agency. She takes two steps—criticizing existing media theory ("cybertheory," as she defines it) and discussing the "interests served by thinking of the Net in terms of a public sphere"—that can be seen as a critique of ideology.[32] Theories of the internet criticized by Dean can be summarized as those whose authors have various and not always justified expectations of the internet as public sphere. The problem lies either in defining such expectations or in defining the public sphere, or in defining the internet, or all of these. Thus, the supposed impossibility of the internet as public sphere lies in the mistakes inherent in theories discussed by Dean—which weakens her statement, as by criticizing some texts, she does not accomplish the task of actually demonstrating the impossibility of the internet as public sphere. One can still very well imagine theories with more adequate definitions of the public sphere and internet, allowing us to solve the equation Dean sees as impossible.

A logical and far more persuasive deduction of the impossibility of equating the internet with the public sphere could be shown by demonstrating the necessary *pars pro toto* mistake involved in such assessment. The internet, as an environment of communication, can be seen as one element of the mixed and far more complex territory of the public sphere, which even in Habermas's theory consists of sharing opinions and discussing matters of the common, which thus involves agents who those matters as well as certain ontologies, epistemologies and worldviews, locations (not just of the internet, whatever we believe it is), humans or other agents, the reproductive labor necessary to make such communication possible in the first place, as well as the technological production and maintenance of its elements, which involves humans. Externalizing the internet of the plethora of things, social relations and the commons in order to claim that it is or should be a public sphere is an obvious conflation, and the notion of ideology or critique is not necessary to reveal such a mistake, although these can help. However, taking such a separated notion of the internet for granted only adds to the ideological reproduction Dean aims to dismantle.

The concept of ideology is, on the other hand, necessary to the second part of Dean's argument—one I find far more interesting— namely, to discuss the interests served by the idea that the internet could be a public sphere. This part of her essay shows the implication of the concept in maintaining the corporate capitalist system of production, involving dispossession, oppression, alienation and exploitation, to name just the central factors. Dean's statement that "publicity, in other words, is the ideology of technoculture" is a great reminder of the deep involvement of the media, and the internet is no exception when it comes to maintaining corporate capitalism.[33] It is also a classical perspective—Adorno and Horkheimer wrote about television and radio as fulfilling the same role of supporting capitalism. Apart from the obvious repetition of the classic critical statement disclosing the media as agents of corporate powers, does such critique of ideology bring anything new? I argue yes—by dismantling the hopes some theorists and activists invested in new media, it points to the deeply ideological character of the public sphere and its conceptualization. However, as a media critique, it is, I believe, in many ways dated, as even in the 1960s and 1970s, media theorists successfully overthrew the homogeneous ontology of information networks as well as the notion of the uninterrupted transmission of the message, in a supposedly linear trajectory, which lies at the core of Dean's argument. Her article's main flaw, in my view, lies in the implicit foreclosure of any forms of resisting media practices, as well as a blunt rejection of the very possibility of media activism, which the #BlackProtest in Poland or #MeToo globally have effectively contradicted. The notion of ideology, central too in Kluge and Negt's *Public Sphere and Experience*, eradicates any prospects of counter-activism in the capitalist mediasphere. I think such generalizations allow the perpetuation of the very ideology they target.

Jodi Dean's analysis is a perfect wakeup call for all those idealizing the internet, who forget about its corporate entanglements and forms of ownership that practically exclude the free exchange of goods, ideas and resistance. However, her analysis is on many levels biased and inaccurate when it comes to the specifics of media, the internet and the public sphere, so that it collapses under its own unreadiness to "get one's hands dirty," as Raunig nicely puts it. A theoretical choice of using a big quantifier while discussing politics, media and the public sphere always already assumes the impossibility of a critical voice. The case of Althusser—par excellence a theorist of ideology, a distant teacher of Žižek, and an inspiring figure for Dean herself—should be a reminder here. The position of a scholar, and a critic of ideology, is always one where the ideological cluster is the most dense. Only the class struggle changes politics. By taking the position of a critic of ideology in an absolute way, and as we have seen, Dean takes no hostages; she consciously extracts herself from the social field she is analyzing, uncritically granting herself the privileged position of external observer. More importantly, by such exteriority a privilege of uncritical generalization is formed, one that allows, for example, an analysis of media that simply is not accurate.

Luckily, this is not a mistake of Hardt and Negri, whose biopolitical understanding of the rebellious multitude does not remove the abstract theory from the discussed social realm. Their analysis of biopolitical labor, earlier depicted to some extent as "immaterial labor," remains in manifold relations with the current studies on technologies, media and labor, thus allowing generalizations of a much more accurate nature than those provided by Dean. In the book she co-edited with Paul Passavant, where various essays criticizing Negri and Hardt's project are compiled, she still references the early formulation, "immaterial labor," and perhaps this criticism was one of the factors leading to Negri and Hardt's transition toward biopolitical labor, which occurred in *Multitudes* and further books of the *Empire* series. However, the critique of the *Empire* project she offers still bears the unnecessary burden of ideology understood in absolute terms. It is also formulated in discussion with the concept of communicative capitalism that Dean has developed over some years now, and it therefore follows her focus on media and communication, which is not so central in *Empire,* although—as Dean rightly claims—it is definitely present as a key aspect of capitalism.

In the discussion offered by Dean in her own chapter of *The Empire's New Clothes*, she emphasizes one of the fundamental contradictions of Negri and Hardt's project—namely that of the insubordinate, rebellious multitude versus the overwhelming Empire. It is the central contradiction of poststructuralism, not solely one present in *Empire*, thus the problem should not be assigned to this book only. Also, this notion is in fact quite central in Marx, Lukács and the critical tradition, wherein the more there is oppression, suddenly the less there is to lose for the oppressed to revolt, yet nothing explains how such revolt might even be conceptualized in the world fully organized by industrial capitalism and its ideological apparatuses. I think solely attributing such a fundamental problem to Negri and Hardt seems somewhat unfair, and thus the following argument, which focuses on one specific aspect of the depicted contradiction—namely the emancipatory use of media by the multitude—seems weakened by the far more general nature of the controversy. Yet in the chapter, Dean rightly connects such notions as the spectacle, in its totality—as depicted by Debord—with the logical implication, which for her is the insurmountable nature of the reign of image. She chooses Agamben's take on Debord and avoids pointing to the contradictions of, say, the community to come and the state of exception or the subversive power of *détournement* versus the society of the spectacle. In defense of Negri and Hardt, I would emphasize that their work on the biopolitics of the multitude has similar problems as the resisting subjects in the mentioned theories. However, while the multitude seems to embrace long-term, collective goals, the striking individualism of Debord's *flâneuse* leaves the prospects of any group action, let alone party politics, out of the available spectrum.

The somewhat forgotten motivation of the multitude to rebel and subvert neoliberal capitalism is obviously rooted in resistance to oppression. It has classical Marxist origins, and thus it does not differ from the main narrative of leftist political theory. However, the possibilities of subversion, alternative and disruption are—and here Negri and Hardt provide quite generously—rooted in collaboration. In work, resistance, experience and rebellion, in all their affective involvements, and affect is not just mere "feeling" here, it is—as in Spinoza—the organization of bodies, as the common pursues its radical developments. The immanent ontology allows us to see the extent to which these developments are corroded by commodification; however, it does open ways for radical affects to lead toward inventive projects.

As in McLuhan's formulation of "the medium is the message," in Dean's proposition, "circulation of the message is value," and its content can be ignored. How to understand the popularity of the #MeToo hashtag and protests, legal actions and cultural changes that resulted of it? How to explain the #BlackProtest in Poland and the massive women's demonstrations, as well as the rejection of the complete ban of abortion in the Parliament? Circulation? No, that would be a simplification, perhaps somehow understandable in the context of #MeToo in the United States, but completely inadequate in Poland. I believe that another *pars pro toto* appears in Dean's understanding of media functioning, one that externalizes corporate interests and then expands them so that it covers the whole of media work. The fact that corporations profit off protests neither allows us to radically reduce the political implications of the protests nor to ignore them. I will return to this problem after some examples of "older" media activism from the distant turn of the twenty-first century.

Among the subversive strategies mentioned in Negri and Hardt's *Empire*, yet not provided with examples, is culture jamming (in addition to other strategies concentrated on the media). I would like to review some of these strategies before discussing the internet and the feminist movement today, which will close the media-focused section of this chapter. Resistance to and *détournement* of media messages have been highlights of several social movements in recent years, as Naomi Klein shows in her book *No Logo*, offering several examples of such actions. They were perhaps most important in the alterglobalization movement, as movement participants hacked commercial and political communications and made them into critical or disruptive messages. In the following section, I share examples of media activism, arguing for a diversified theory of media action and acceptance of the different strategies and aims that media activism can have. In the subsequent discussion of the internet in the counterpublics, I believe such analysis of earlier media activism is in place, and we probably do not need to invent media strategies for social media anew. Radical social movements often resign from learning from past experiences, which is a bad practice not just from my perspective, as someone who tried to build and preserve radical archives, but also from the view of anyone willing to effectively oppose corporate capitalism. The examples offered here should thus be seen as an integral part of the discussion of media and politics, which cannot externalize the internet or present it as separated from other media, nor only focus on the experiences of one generation (this creates a sense of exceptionality, which is at best pretentious and at worst exclusivist and essentializing).

One great example of a culture jamming practice was the sudden appearance in 2001 of leaflets advertising Lufthansa's flights as 30 percent cheaper if passengers agree to fly on an aircraft where deported persons are transported. These leaflets, distributed mainly in Germany, brought public attention to the problem of violence always present in deportations and—as customers stormed travel agencies to purchase the tickets—also led to lengthy explanations on the side of Lufthansa as to why the company agreed to collaborate with the state on such a dangerous mission. The No Border network then informed the public that several deported persons die on deportation flights every year due to the violence they experience from state functionaries while being put on such flights or while flying.

Another example involved a poster that appeared in Warsaw in 2001 advertising free and unlimited access to American visas for Polish people during George Bush's visit in Poland. During the three days of his visit, Bush was asked several times about the United States' visa policies, and specifically about Polish citizens' right to visit his country, and it was rather embarrassing when at first his response revealed that he had no clue about the fact that such visas are required.

These are cases of disruptions in the commodified flow of information that, while they bring at least a smile to the tired faces of cultural critics, activists and some other groups, do not cause more systematic social change, and they were rightly criticized for that. The praise for such swift and elegant expressions of social criticism, however, should not be fully dismantled. Social movements need to gather some sense of hope, otherwise despair dominates even in moments of true opportunity to bring change. I agree with all those critics of culture jamming who contest the fetishization of such moments of countercultural glory, allowing them to become the essence of anticapitalist agency. Such fetishization dismantles any interest in systematic critical and social work; while providing much-needed optimism, it also crushes any efforts to strengthen and diversify the movement and allows an easy co-optation of resistance by corporations. It is similar to the blunt enthusiasm many social critics had for the internet and 3D printing, which were supposed to free us all, and somehow they did not, instead becoming fundamental elements of the biopolitical capitalist machine. However, I do not think that critique of ideology—be it offered by Dean or the one from

Dialectic of Enlightenment or another, constitutes a sufficient tool to dismantle capitalist powers.

There are other, more systematic disruptions and resistance strategies that bring more long-term effects, but only if practiced by groups in a very disciplined way. One of them was applied in Poland, and it consisted of spreading feminist messaging in ways that allowed for acceptance of the movement in times when it was largely depreciated. I recall a very popular public TV show in Poland, *Warto rozmawiać* (*It's Worth Discussing*) led by a conservative journalist who always exoticized, diminished and ridiculed the left and feminism. In 2003, a group of feminist activists went to a taping of this show as guests and hijacked it. This led, among other repercussions, to my neighbors and local shop assistants declaring that "We weren't feminists before seeing the show, but we sure are now!" One of my neighbors actually gave me a bottle of homemade sherry to congratulate the audacity of our feminist crew. Similar groups of activists have been participating in media programs, giving interviews and otherwise influencing the media with a comprehensive feminist vision, assertive yet not aggressive messaging and a big smile on their faces. It has worked largely because it has been the practice of some dozens of activists, who decided to transform media images of feminism, consciously taking on the role of feminist media officers.

Another example of feminists using the media effectively was in 2007, during the big nurses' strike. Many installed themselves in front of the government headquarters of Aleje Ujazdowskie in Warsaw in tents, hence the name "White Town" that was given to the protest.[34] I felt especially committed to supporting them as their protest began on the same day as my PhD defense and my doctoral research was Marxist-feminist through and through. I visited the camp on a daily basis and on occasion, I overheard that they were desperate. After two weeks none of their demands had been met and there was still no media attention. They felt, and rightly so, that without press coverage their protest would be seen as basically benign, nothing for the government to worry about. Upon hearing this, I had a genius idea. Why not use the brilliant work of Joanna Rajkowska, *Greetings from Jerusalem Avenue*? For those unfamiliar with this critically acclaimed intervention, it is composed of a big artificial palm tree conveniently located in the Rondo de Gaulla in the city center. Why not hang a big nurse's hat (a white rectangle with a black, horizontal stripe in the middle) from the top of this tree? The palm tree was undergoing maintenance, and the artist immediately agreed. She also wanted to help but was busy with the maintenance. At first, the activity of painting a black stripe on a white rectangle felt idiotic. Yet I soon realized that this was also actually a small tribute to Kazimir Malevich and his *Black Square*, a painting I admire. And so, titling it *Tribute to Malevich*, my own painting became a declaration of the suprematist conviction that the social is what we should really care about. With this optimistic thought, I finished the nurse's hat (again, a black stripe in the middle of a white surface) and the next morning it was hung on the palm tree in the center of Warsaw. This galvanized the Polish media and the nurses got the attention they so needed. There were tears of joy from the protesters and people passing by, which was actually very sweet. This action clearly would not fit in Habermas's or Kluge and Negt's political paradigm, as the nurse's hat was so heterogeneous, transversal and multilayered. Their analyses flatten all cultural representations in media as victims of commodification, rendering them incapable of grasping the effects of *Tribute to Malevich* or even the process of its making. (I am grateful to the artist Joanna Rajkowska for fully supporting this action.)

It is necessary to stress that countercultures today, as well as large parts of public debate, have actually moved from media to cultural events and institutions. The most interesting debates concerning the problems of art today are usually initiated not by the media or academia, but by protests and conflicts concerning "what is art?," "what is good art?" or—my favorite doubt repeated in the neoliberal economy— "should the taxpayers' money finance this crap?" The activism for or against such art-focused discussion, which usually begins with some effort to censor an artwork, often becomes very popular and multidimensional, thus breaking the bubble of specialists or "the cultured." In these controversies, which are rather frequent in Poland, we hear perhaps more interesting statements than those expounded at academic conferences.[35] Similarly, in the case of workers' rights, and as exemplified by the nurses and their hat, debates initiated by or due to social protest have been the most effective. I believe the role of media in those cases is at least twofold: they document and disseminate the events, obviously transforming them according to their political and commercial lines; however, as in every cultural production, these processes can be *détourned*, hijacked or ideologically appropriated. The little *Tribute to Malevich* action spoke for itself, to a large extent, and it would be very hard to appropriate its meaning and transform it in the service of some commercial or pro-governmental program. While not everyone in Poland is familiar with Malevich, everyone knows what a nurse's hat looks like, and they obviously identified my painting as such and immediately linked it to the ongoing protest.

The examples of media activism depicted above are a necessary element in the discussion of today's media activism and the political role of the internet for women's protests and feminist politics. These discussions often seem detached from the prior history of media activism, thus reducing the potential of certain arguments, strategies or forms of agency. In what follows, I argue that as much as the internet indeed *is not the public sphere*, some of its parts and functions allow space for counterpublics and their maintenance outside of street protests and other forms of direct action, and thus it should be valued as an important element in the maintenance of progressive politics.

The last of the aforementioned examples of media activism is an action that went viral, but first it built a real-life connection between the artwork and the social movement of nurses. It was meant to be mediated by various televisions and other media, and it fully succeeded in doing that. It also allowed direct support for the members of the nurses' strike, who were resigned and desperate—it gave them much needed hope, immediately and without any risk on their part. It also gave me and other participants an opportunity to take effective action with immediate gratitude and symbolic gratifi-cation—one of the rare occasions when such things happen; twenty years of activism and a conscious decision to stay involved, at least to some extent, teaches one to cherish such exceptional moments. This is, by the way, something for social critics to embrace—their highly privileged lives often do not require such little satisfactions, allowing splendid isolation and clean hands at once. Unfortunately—with academia quickly precarizing, this will soon be something to learn for more of us—how to sustain resistance, not just how to best criticize the corporate means of communication.

These core elements of action can also be located in other examples provided—the sense of solidarity, disruption of typical media content, new political debates, a possibility to share—and all of these elements constitute vital elements of activists' life, most of them also bring necessary hope to those desperate in their sense of solitude, pain, oppression and isolation. The message transmitted is: you are not alone. Only a particularly vicious person or someone who never was in desperate need of solidarity can ignore the importance of such messages. The fact that they bolster corporate capitalist powers should not be ignored, but it is not the only element in this complex situation.

In such heterogeneous perspectives on media, the internet included, corporate profits are not immediately taken as those which "take it all." They take the most, yes, and unfortunately so, but for the maintenance of our integrity and resistance, for the sake of building genuinely international collaborations across the globe, we are doomed to corporate information systems, just as we do not produce our food, clothes and other things on our own, with that small exception of people who decide to do so, but they are a minority, as are the circles of people who manage to avoid corporate internet networks, at least in the West.

The #MeToo campaign, by far the largest and most important feminist campaign in recent years and largely happening online, led to revolutionary changes in several fields. First, quite concretely, it allowed women, their lawyers and the courts of justice to finally challenge sexual harassment in workplaces. In almost every country in Europe, Japan, the United States, Canada and many countries in South America, several particularly visible sectors of production, such as media, universities and corporations, have witnessed women accusing men (in very rare cases—also women) of abuse. More importantly, though, people around the globe have learned about the scale of sexual harassment in the most persuasive way—by witnessing the avalanche in 2017 of declarations of suffered abuse by masses of women, some nonbinary people and men that happened online after actress Alyssa Milano accused Hollywood producer Harvey Weinstein of sexual assault. As detailed in the previous chapter, the hashtag #MeToo and the campaign was invented much earlier, though, by African American feminist Tarana Burke, who as early as 2006 called for solidarity with harassed women. Tithi Bhattacharia writes about 40,000 women responding to Milano on that day.[36] As many scholars emphasize, we cannot fully grasp the implications of the #MeToo campaign yet. However, some effects can already be seen. In terms of informing the social masses about the scale of this phenomenon, the campaign successfully spread this information, as well as demonstrating that women in our direct proximity experienced violence. Obviously, from the perspective of Jodi Dean, it all does not count, as only the circulation of information, not its content, matters for capital. Similarly, the solidarity structures and messages of hope and support should not count—and these were plenty, as witnessed by countless internet users, who declared their experiences and got responses, as well as a sense of belonging, while many of them had previously thought their painful experience was exceptional. Such support fuels further activism or even persistence in staying alive, and it helps in overcoming depression, post-traumatic stress disorders and other trauma-related repercussions. In one of her letters, Rosa Luxemburg wrote about despair and how it is a comfort only available for the truly privileged, as the oppressed are constantly struggling, and cannot afford resignation.[37] In such constant struggle—and most of us are living in struggle, not in privilege—moments of hope, solidarity and support are everything, and they provide care and ideas of change as well.

Once again, though, for critics focused on information's circulation, that would not count. I would like to take a different position, however, and explain why it does count. First and foremost—we have never been many. Well, I have a family-injected sense of solidarity already from the "solidarity" movement—I grew up in it. But most of my friends and colleagues do not have such a sense of belonging to a large-scale social movement. Their hopes for ever having such an experience are substantially lower than mine, as is their hope for a different form of social organization. It does matter whether we have such experiences, and for many participants of #MeToo, that was it— for the first time in their lives, many women felt a sense of community. In Chapter 2, I depicted the recent women's protests in Poland and the mechanism that led from a hashtag, #BlackProtest, to the streets. It is likely that most women who wrote about their experiences of harassment within the #MeToo campaign did not participate in demonstrations. But maybe some of them did?

Today's main issue—to a large extent, inviting the critique of ideology to come back and have some popcorn—is obviously the huge backlash after the massive expression of women's solidarity online. London-based feminist writer Laurie Penny claims that every feminist author she knows has received violent threats at least once.[38] Various analyses of internet discussions after 2016 have focused on the unprecedented amount of antifeminist and misogynist voices, some of which directly target women or feminist groups. In her book *Kill All Normies*, Angela Nagle presents a dark image of the internet and recent online battles, where ultraconservatives, racists, sexist men, the alt-right and incels form a global network of extremely effective alliances and succeed in pushing back, terrorizing and trolling feminist and otherwise progressive messages.[39] She argues, quite persuasively, that this conservative digital revolution is leaderless and thus embraces antinormative, conflicted and inconsistent symbols, cleverly hijacking anarchic expressions and values from the left-leaning and progressive countercultures of prior decades to gain hegemony for the right on the internet. Between the lines of her sometimes brilliant observations of the connections between supposedly disconnected persons and online communities, Nagle details the overwhelming domination of violence and misogyny on the internet, an image that can easily be undermined by the earlier images of the #MeToo campaigns and other feminist online activism. The rather minoritarian groups following such nihilist ideas as those of Nick Land suddenly seem overwhelmingly present in online debates. This image—cleverly constructed as it is—cannot hold; however, it does provide an important insight into how antinormative positions have infiltrated the right. It also has obvious flaws, such as blaming the popularity of poststructuralist feminism and queer, pro-trans politics for the expansion of the antinormative trends on the right.

A somewhat opposing narrative about the internet and the horrifying victories of the contemporary alt-right has been offered by Jen Schradie, who, in *The Revolution that Wasn't*, shows the failure of hopes for digital liberation.[40] Her sometimes meticulous analysis of various social organizations active in North Carolina, based on several years of analysis of these movements, focusing on their online activity, clearly shows a far stronger agency of such kind on the right. Schradie rightly argues that the internet mirrors the existing social divisions, and only seldom, if ever, allows those who lack cultural or economic capital to gain it by means available on the internet. She carefully examines various assumptions from earlier, cyber-optimistic decades, only to discover that economic prosperity, established role divisions and a clear focus allow for much more online effectiveness than the scattered, disorganized and impoverished backgrounds of many active on the left. The study offered in *The Revolution That Wasn't* thus can be seen as directly opposing Nagle's perspective.

I think these two narratives complement each other, although it should also be noted that they are very different in style and quality—Nagle's sharp sense of observation is nevertheless weaker than Schradie's scientific method in addressing the constraints of the internet today. They capture different aspects of the same process. They detail people like the organized, financially secure conservative farmer who systematically challenges local progressive feminists through, say, two hours per day of constant trolling and thirty minutes of supporting Trump on Twitter; and his friends from a local Tea Party branch (this example is my invention somewhat based on Schradie's book, but not taken from it), who imagine themselves as some postmodern lone cowboys of the right, Milo-styled bad boys of the internet and so on. Psychoanalysis, as well as cultural theory, explain how the ego-ideal and everyday practice may form a conflicted yet powerful bond between these individuals, allowing the successful production of subjects. Here, in online activism, the hiatus between the imagined heroes, the anti-Normies of the alt-right, constitute a perfect match for the Scout-inspired daily routine. More importantly, perhaps the only way of explaining the efficiency of the alt-right—as Žižek does whenever he speaks of the Yugoslav Army—is how anarchistic, vulgar and uncontrolled ego-ideals sustain the orderly daily actions of the church-loving traditionalists worldwide, providing inspiration and a dream in which to live.

The analysis of internet behaviors and subcultures clearly needs psychoanalysis, and perhaps it also needs dialectics. Otherwise, it ends up projecting a flat world supposedly free of contradictions, where there is no such thing as the subconscious and human actions are conveniently rooted solely in past actions and choices, disconnected from their imaginary contexts and affects. Online agency, be it feminist, alt-right or any other, cannot be reduced to its supposed "success" or "failure" because, as with any other human agency, it usually fulfills someone's needs, limits someone's freedom and opens some possibilities. From this perspective, the current antifeminist backlash, as well as the triumphs of the alt-right and conservatives online, are moments in history preceded by other moments and waiting for others to come. They cannot and should not be seen as the internet's last word, and most often their understanding is limited by a tendency to treat as absolute how the internet's "now" seems omnipresent, as well as a need to reduce online agency to one dimension, be it corporate interests, antinormative dreams fueling the imaginations of the traditionalists or class organization in internet activism.

Understanding ideology as a process in which contradictions, mistakes and failures are not merely happening but also have far-reaching consequences, including those of a radical nature, might be a way out of the flattening tendency, the reduction of every historical scenario to only one end. Perhaps Hardt and Negri's efforts to express the emancipatory potential of, as well as the deep involvement of new technologies in, biopolitical neoliberal production allow a better understanding of the internet than the concept of ideology that erases the very possibility of embracing resistance within communication capital.

It is necessary to emphasize that counterpublics of the common are unimaginable without feminist critique of the public/private divide, of the neoliberal economy and of the backlash appearing wherever women's rights seem to have been won, including after #MeToo. The feminist critique of precarization, including the analysis of Isabell Lorey, on one hand, and Silvia Federici, on the other, clearly show the gendered aspects of neoliberal capitalism, in which women and immigrants are left with the care obligations no longer fulfilled by the state and/or employers. Their analysis of the European subject as always keeping its "others" in precarity (Lorey) and of the necessity and difficulty of the care workers' strike (Federici) both demonstrate how the contemporary version of capitalism imposes the reproduction of traditional gender roles even in supposedly emancipated societies. These critiques, combined with those of the patriarchal norms of the political, most significant in maintaining the public/ private divide (Pateman), those criticizing the masculinist reading of political agency and that of women (Honig) and the intertwining of gender and colonial politics in what Gloria Anzaldúa called the obligation of a "straight story" together make contemporary political agency—be it that of the common and the one performed within counterpublics or both combined—deeply marked by feminist insights and practices. These contestations and transformations of the model of the political, combined with the mass feminist protests—often fueled by ordinary gestures such as globally used hashtags like #MeToo, #YesAllWomen or #RapedAndNeverReported and selfie posting and black clothes, as in the Black Protests in Poland, or the pink hats in the United States or the green scarfs in Argentina—revitalize the idea of a general transformation of the public sphere and with it a sense of awakening a new feminist politics in various counterpublics. These movements are antifascist in challenging the authoritarian, biopolitical forms of states of exception, appearing in slightly different versions in different countries due to the rise of the radical right-wing governments coming to power.

The feminist protests are not something else than, beyond or on the margin of contemporary politics. In recent years they reshaped our image of mass protest, our vision of political demands and what follows: our theory and practice of political agency in general. As I have argued in the preceding chapters, the emergence of this new and massive feminist agency is a clear signal not solely of the fact, that—as Foucault wrote—wherever there is repression, there is also resistance, but that women are no longer accepting the constant relegation of our oppression to the invisible and supposedly "apolitical" private. Personal becomes political not solely on feminist banners or manifestos, but in the daily practice of institutions, workplaces, courts and the media, which means that our old, tired conceptual frameworks of the political need to be reworked in order to follow the dynamic of today's politics.

This means that the new forms of reorganization and revolution to be invented, as Negri and Hardt argue in the closing parts of *Assembly*, perhaps are already here in the counterpublics of the feminist commons in revolt. They consist of dismantling the public/private division not solely on the level of ownership, but also in the ways they shape the conditions of political agency. It means that production should be understood as the core site of the political and involve reproductive labor. This includes, but is not limited to, reproductive rights and all the labor that needs to be done for the production of subjects.

When the doctrine of the state of exception becomes most powerful, dictating the politics of Western and Eastern countries, at least in Europe and the Americas, and sweeping the politics of the left away, it means only that we need to rehearse new forms of antifascist politics, fail, and learn to fail better as we try to transgress the limitations of contemporary models. This means revisiting the historical transformations of the public sphere, not in a nostalgic desire for peace and tranquility, but to unlearn our assumptions about who can do politics and how, and to revisit the times in which the egalitarian political line was strong. It does not mean copying past solutions, but instead observing strategies and practices in order to overcome the neoliberal individualism imposed as the only model of agency in the last thirty years.

4

Weak Resistance:
Beyond the Heroic Model of Political Agency

Feminist art theory has contested the male-dominated politics of representation. Several important interventions in this context have been taken by feminist scholars and activists, one of the most famous in Linda Nochlin's essay "Why Have There Been No Great Women Artists?", published in 1971. Spoiler alert: there could not have been any, because the very figure of artist was shaped according to male socialization and masculine roles.[1] The question does not allow us to address such reasoning, thus condemning those who seek the answer to search in the wrong direction.

A similar question could be asked regarding politics. Today such a question would already sound out of place in countries like Finland, where the 2020 government is composed of five parties run by women and a prime minister who is a thirty-five-year-old woman and a child of a lesbian couple. However, in many other countries, sadly, such a question is not completely dated, and it could be built in a similar way to that about women artists: "Why Have There Been No Great Women Politicians?" The historically accurate answer, also one politically hopeful, would be: because the most popular models of political agency have been shaped according to masculine socialization and male role models. In both sectors, women have also been quite explicitly, often by law, excluded. Nochlin rightly argued that in order to answer such questions, one should prove the opposite by finding examples of women who actually were artists or politicians—as the answer to my question above would suggest. The task is to turn the tables and shift the perspective, otherwise the conditions of women's exclusion from various sectors of human life will remain invisible.

The notion of weak resistance, which I have been working on for years, introduces such a shift in the context of counterpublics' political agency.[2] This concept embraces various aspects of the perspectives and agencies of different oppressed and marginalized groups while also capturing certain elements of the dynamics of the multitude becoming the common (possibly in revolt). In my research, it proved to be an interesting shift from the patriarchal, heroic vision of agency, still so expansively dominating our political imagination and theory. It is to some extent inspired by Walter Benjamin, whose idea of "weak messianism," briefly mentioned in his "Theses on the Philosophy of History," remains inspiring for several philosophers, such as Gianni Vattimo, whose theory of "weak thought" fueled some currents of deconstruction; Jacques Derrida, whose *Specters of Marx* explains the non-mystical signification of Benjamin's idea; or Boris Groys, whose essay "The Weak Universalism" argues for a revision of the understanding of avant-garde.[3] In this chapter I discuss its main elements and consider some other inspirations, such as Jack Halberstam's *The Queer Art of Failure,* Vaclav Havel's *The Power of the Powerless,* James Scott's *Weapons of the Weak* and the notion of "territory" in Gilles Deleuze and Félix Guattari's *A Thousand Plateaus.* Methodologically, this chapter perhaps owes most to the work of Donna Haraway, particularly her perspective on situated knowledges, the cyborg and the Capitalocene. I also consider *The Xenofeminist Manifesto* to be an important contribution to the field of feminist politics and theory.[4] These references, as well as the examples I discuss, taken from politics, theory, art history and even sport, lead to the conclusion that we must revise the image of political agency, and this is particularly necessary from a feminist point of view. But in the context of counter publics of the common, we might be tempted to ask: what kind of political agency fuels people? How do we understand the inconsistent, contradictory, conflicted, sometimes openly mistaken movements of the common? How can proletarians, women, Blacks and other marginalized groups do politics? (Which they do, there is no doubt about that.) Should their agency remain conveniently invisible in order for politics, even progressive politics, to remain exclusive? Or can we perhaps imagine a world where politics can be discussed with adequate concepts, and by adequate I do not mean those "corresponding to reality," as in Aristotle's mistaken notion of truth, but those of which the complexity actually accounts for the diversity of political agency already active in the contradictory conditions of neoliberal capitalism as well as those foreclosed or marginalized in those conditions, together with the spectrum of those political acts that we can (today more hardly than ever) also imagine.

The notion of weak resistance undermines the "easy fix" strategy, rightly criticized by Donna Haraway in *Staying with the Trouble*. She depicts the current crises of the Capitalocene as provoking several insufficient or mistaken responses: the "techno-fixes," which are ideas of tools that act as fast remedies to the symptoms of the crisis and are nevertheless portrayed as solutions to its causes, and depressive refusal to take any action.[5] Haraway's solution consists of staying with the trouble and building networks and collaborative solutions across various distinctions and even species.

It is worth mentioning, in the context of the discussions of media—in this book and more generally—that Haraway's alternative of two erroneous versions of political agency has many historical predecessors, structurally; it also resembles the contradiction between the positions taken by Hardt and Negri in their theory of the Empire and that offered by Jodi Dean, as well as Slavoj Žižek and other scholars, concerning engagement in contemporary politics. The controversy between Jean Baudrillard and Susan Sontag over the staging of Beckett's *Waiting for Godot* in Sarajevo in 1993, during the city's siege by the Serbians, was much simpler. It featured the French intellectual, who asked to "leave them [the Bosnians] in peace," and Sontag, who declared that she could not just sit in New York doing nothing.[6] The dispute included Baudrillard referring to Sontag as one of those irresponsible intellectuals from the West, who are "weak," while the besieged Bosnians are "strong," and this is another reason for bringing in this example. Interestingly, in Baudrillard's 1995 article in *Liberation*, the Bosnians are depicted as "strong" in their ability to endure suffering. Clearly, the otherwise useful notion

of simulacrum is not necessary to describe reality; sometimes depicting such shifts allows an understanding of the liquidity of today's
information. Baudrillard also (in)famously stated that the Gulf War
never happened.[7] As acute as such observation might seem, it also
enables various misreadings of political agency. It also legitimizes
mistaken facts and undocumented deductions, and after the panic of
the "post-truth" era, we are probably more than skeptical about
Baudrillard's claims.

In her notes after the staging of *Godot* in Sarajevo, Sontag noted:

> When, in April, I heard the French intellectual Andre Glucksmann,
> on his twenty-four-hour trip to Sarajevo, explain to the people of
> Sarajevo who had come to his press conference that "war is now a
> media event," and "wars are won or lost on TV," I thought to
> myself: try telling that to all the people here who have lost their
> arms and legs. But there is a sense in which Glucksmann's indecent
> statement was on the mark. It's not that war has completely
> changed its nature, and is only or principally a media event, but
> that the media's coverage is a principal object of attention, and the
> very fact of media attention sometimes becomes the main story.[8]

Sontag had no trouble understanding media politics; however, her
ability to approach the stakes of her journey was not significant, just
as her somewhat blunt acceptance of the NATO intervention did not
capture the complexity of the situation and the complicity of Western
reactions to the war in Yugoslavia. And yet, after several decades, her
effort to perpetuate cultural productions in a city under siege for
several years might seem more compelling than the efforts to with-
draw from any actions offered by Baudrillard.

Instead of trying to champion one strategy over the other, I would
like to understand both of them as failures in response to the war
conflict. Both Sontag's and Baudrillard's positions are captured in a
dichotomy imposed by the system of colonial capitalism, where
distinctions are kept not just between social classes and professions,
but also geographical regions, and the hegemony of the West is
perpetuated also by its charitable involvements internationally. In

this perspective, both forms of alienation—that of unmediated action as well as that of detached meditation—are natural repercussions of the globalized division of labor and thus problematically uncritical to their own conditions of possibility. We need to keep in mind that while the notion of solidarity occupies an important place in European sociology, it has been of key value only in the radical left. Solidarity has never been a fundamental political value in liberalism and conservatism, not to mention fascism. Thus, in our political imagination, to a large degree shaped by liberal and conservative political ideologies, solidarity as a form of political agency is not as important as competition, respect, resistance, victory or struggle. Sharing empathy, sustaining or supporting each other, as well as persisting throughout long-term oppression (say, a siege) are not central notions of political theory, and they are also quite marginal in common speech. This makes forms of activism like the one taken by Sontag a peculiarity rather than a "normal" choice. In Chapter 1 I did not mention all of those who supported the activists who were there, whether in prison, hiding or persecuted. Theirs was also a political role; however, there are no concepts, except perhaps that of solidarity or affective labor, to discuss their involvement in a more precise way, allowing us to document their involvement in both historical accounts as well as more theoretical analyses. Obviously, this is a very general problem of political and theoretical narrative, to which we are accustomed, as that from within struggles. The notion of weak resistance is meant to change that and make this kind of exclusion impossible.

Walter Benjamin defined weak messianism as a pact between generations, one allowing solidarity in struggle, and also as a task for historical materialism. Derrida argues for a non-mystical interpretation of this notion, and I believe it to be the correct interpretation, especially in the context of discussing Marxism after 1989. Derrida chose to return to Marx and the concept of weak messianism in a time of the supposed "end of history," so (in)famously announced by Francis Fukuyama, and I believe his choice was not accidental. The triumphant enunciations of the supposed end of communism proved to be timely, however—that was a time of (yet another) defeat of the left, somewhat similar to that we live now, with fascist and ultraconservative politicians taking over in so many countries. The somewhat melancholic yet hopeful reference to the bonds between generations suggests the importance of the historical process, somehow against the focus on the "now," so central in most theories built around the notion of ideology. Such approaches to capitalism, which reduce its historical evolution to a mere reference, often end up fetishizing the current mode, thus giving up the possibilities offered by the processes of learning, unlearning and rehearsal so central in Rosa Luxemburg's critique of imperialism, Marx's critique of political economy or Gayatri Spivak's theory of the subaltern. In their praise of the "event," they smoothly sweep the already marginalized knowledges of the oppressed, thus condemning radical politics for constant repetitions of the same or similar mistakes as well as for an exclusive vision of political agency, where only the already recognized, hegemonic modes are perceptible. In this, the approach of Dean and Žižek to revolution forecloses an appearance of the opposition to capitalism substantially different from the power structures we have known in it within the conditions it has established and imposed. Negri and Hardt, with their focus on immanence, also risk a similar mistake; however, the perspective of a transition of the multitude toward the common within a revolution more so allows an embrace of history, that of the excluded, marginalized and oppressed, as well as the cracks and dissonances announcing change.

James Scott offered a very important analysis of what I call weak resistance in his seminal study *Weapons of the Weak*, built from some ten years of research with peasants' movements in Southeast Asia.[9] Scott's analysis embraces the ordinary and grassroots character of peasant mobilizations and their weakness as subjects without any power or position. As he argues, due to the impossibility of organizing politically in classical ways, the subaltern classes usually focus on concrete, everyday matters and choose ordinary strategies of resistance, which are perhaps the most effective in the long run. Scott concludes: "[The mobilizations of the weak] require little or no coordination or planning; they make use of implicit understandings and informal networks; they often represent a form of individual self-help; they typically avoid any direct, symbolic confrontation with authority."[10] The examples of mobilization Scott analyzes are not solely concerned with basic matters, as he explains: "The struggle between rich and poor in Sedaka [a Malaysian village, fictional name] is not merely a struggle over work, property rights, grain, and cash. It is also a struggle over the appropriation of symbols, a struggle over how the past and present shall be understood and labeled, a struggle to identify causes and assess blame, a contentious effort to give partisan meaning to local history." It is important to note that without some kind of mediation—be it through political organizations or state institutions—such movements would not realize their goals. Critics of Scott's study emphasize this unacknowledged aspect, and rightly so. Also, the supposed lack of organizational structures was in some cases transformed into new forms of organizing. Regardless of these weaknesses in Scott's work, its key aspect was his effort to document forms of political agency that remain invisible in the classic lens of historical account—which prioritizes heroic fighters over peaceful protesters, men over women and the strong over the weak— to instead allow us to imagine counterpublics of the common.

An interesting model of everyday resistance was proposed in Václav Havel's famous essay *The Power of the Powerless*.[11] It allows a reading of Solidarność as a nonheroic and yet radical event. Zbigniew Bujak, one of the key figures of Solidarność and a factory worker from Ursus, emphasizes the importance of Havel's text for the events of 1980. He recalls it in rather heroic terms nevertheless:

> Then came the essay by Havel. Reading it gave us the theoretical underpinnings for our activity. It maintained our spirits; we did not give up, and a year later—in August 1980—it became clear that the party apparatus and the factory management were afraid of us. We mattered. And the rank and file saw us as leaders of the movement. When I look at the victories of Solidarity, and of Charter 77, I see in them an astonishing fulfillment of the prophecies and knowledge contained in Havel's essay.[12]

Havel offered "an examination of the potential of the 'powerless'" arguing that it "can only begin with an examination of the nature of power in the circumstances in which these powerless people operate."[13] He depicted the existing global political system around 1978 as so overwhelming that nothing could supposedly be done within its norms and structures, and a sense of "dissent" so strong that it needs to be expressed. In the opening paragraph, Havel paraphrases the first lines of *The Communist Manifesto*:

> A spectre is haunting eastern Europe: the spectre of what in the West is called "dissent." This spectre has not appeared out of thin air. It is a natural and inevitable consequence of the present histor-ical phase of the system it is haunting. It was born at a time when this system, for a thousand reasons, can no longer base itself on the unadulterated, brutal, and arbitrary application of power, elimi-nating all expressions of nonconformity. What is more, the system has become so ossified politically that there is practically no way for such nonconformity to be implemented within its official structure.[14]

Havel's narrative depicts the world as governed by two superpowers, possessing claims to historical and ideological legitimacy that are so strong they do not need any "heroic" confirmations. Havel decided to call the world he inhabited a *post-totalitarian system*. He suggested a certain automatism, with which both ordinary citizens and state rulers function in a completely mechanic way. The image of a green-grocer suddenly contesting the status quo, central for Havel's essay, is not one of heroic bravery. It comes as a refusal to present a slogan depicted as "a threat to the system not because of any physical or actual power he had, but because his action went beyond itself, because it illuminated its surrounding[s]."[15] Living in truth was Havel's formula for possible political agency of nonheroic resistance in the post-totalitarian system, where "every free expression of life indirectly threatens the post-totalitarian system politically."[16] In 1968, but also in the movement around Charter 77—later depicted as exceptional not merely because it united communists and noncom-munists but because it was "a priori open to anyone," which also constituted an important aspect of Solidarność ten years later—the political confrontation was not happening, Havel argued, between two superpowers. The power is with the state apparatus; the people do not have it. This causes a paradoxical opportunity for those who are not professional politicians to express their dissent in ordinary, "weak" ways.

Genuine politics should therefore happen on the level of everyday life. This sounds strikingly similar to the preoccupation of Negt and Kluge with the lived experience of proletarians in their theory of counterpublics. As well, Havel's distinction between what he called "genuine politics" and what for him should happen on the level of "life" sounds strikingly similar to theories of the "revolution of the everyday," from Vaneigem and Lefebvre to de Certeau and others. Havel's essay was written in 1978 then smuggled into Poland, and in 1979 and 1980 it performed the fantastic task of providing inspiration for political opposition. Havel's depiction of the "power of the powerless," of necessary resistance, done with the smallest gestures, should not be read as an expression of liberal individualism, although this would probably be the political doctrine most attractive for that author. In the closing parts of Havel's essay, we see an image of the resisting grocery salesmen and other people getting together. I believe that this is a very powerful image, and it inspired not only Bujak, but also many others in different places and times. I believe it is reminiscent of James Scott's *Weapons of the Weak* and the protests of peasants in Southeast Asia—these are the protests of the least heroic form imaginable, and yet particularly effective, even in terms of scale.[17] This form of resistance does not involve exceptionality or heroic gestures; it requires persistence and everyday life strategies.

In the opening pages of *The Queer Art of Failure*, Jack Halberstam declares that their book "dismantles the logics of success and failure with which we currently live. Under certain circumstances failing, losing, forgetting, unmaking, undoing, unbecoming, not knowing may in fact offer more creative, more cooperative, more surprising ways of being in the world."[18] With the overwhelming focus on productivity and success so typical of neoliberal capitalism, particularly in times of crisis, mastering failure can perhaps be the way to live, not just to survive. There is also another dimension of failure that I find important: that of learning from the mistakes, insufficiency or flaws of a particular agency/position.

Halberstam's idea of failure as depicted in the book highlights those aspects of resistance to neoliberal capitalism that are not always based upon a conscious decision or political choices, but sometimes happen unintentionally or even against the chosen purpose. In that, Halberstam follows Judith Butler's theory of gender insubordination, where the misfits of the binary identity grid sometimes disturb the performative repetition of the heteromatrix, incidentally subverting it without such intent.[19] As I argue elsewhere while discussing Gerald Raunig's theory of resistance to neoliberal knowledge production modes, such a conceptual framework, where resistance is something wider than just the sum of intended acts, opens far more possibilities for understanding historical as well as future modes of subversion versus classical accounts, which are rooted in rationalist theories of subjectivity.[20] Similarly to Hardt and Negri's multitude, Butler's and Halberstam's gender insubordinates often follow their affective, sometimes perfectly unconscious drives rather than a meticulously prepared plan of some, say, communist party avant-garde, the bourgeois public sphere or male-dominated institutions.

In philosophical discourse, resistance has been portrayed as symptomatic of the negative in the historical panorama, thereby announcing an exception.[21] This definition of the revolution as exceptional, and as produced by extraordinary subjects, suddenly and without a history of mistakes and rehearsals, has been fetishized to an extent that makes it unimaginable for any agency of lesser exceptionality than a genuine avant-garde to cause any social change. Perceived in strictly individualistic terms, such revolution, or even contestation, is only imaginable as caused by some extraordinary agents in a fictional world. Contemporary media depictions of resistance, too, often do not provide a balanced description of the participants in protests, choosing the most extravagant characters and presenting them as leaders, sometimes without any insight into processes within the movements.

A possibility of resistance beyond plan supposedly resembles the spontaneity of revolutionary masses so praised by Luxemburg. We must proceed with caution reading her work, though, because it usually features the process, not some miraculous new beginnings. Luxemburg also emphasized the need to overcome disappointment and embrace failure as a natural element of struggle. As Loralea Michaelis argues:

> [In Luxemburg] we can see more clearly how the experience of failure could make the realization of socialism more rather than less certain, and in terms that refer more directly to the inner situation of the socialist activist than the abstract assurances on which Marx relied: failure occasions the opportunity for deeper learning but, more importantly, it is in the experience of failure that the commitment on which the realization of socialism depends is tested and, in Luxemburg's hands at least, forged.[22]

In her letters from different prisons, Luxemburg emphasized how despair is a luxury that only the privileged can enjoy. Contrary to despair, failure is for her an experience to be embraced, as communist politics will fail spectacularly, and many times, before it can win. Such perspective, focusing on repeating, somehow rehearsing alternatives to capitalism, is a necessary element of weak resistance. Luxemburg's works and speeches on the autonomy of proletarian politics in relation to the German social democrats of her times depict a certain power that comes with failure and weakness.

These remarks do not automatically lead to the replacement of organized structures with chaotic movements or to the notion that politics only proceeds in irrational ways, although it sometimes happens. The notion of counterpublics embraces organized structures as well as the lived experience, which is sometimes chaotic and always affective. In the works of Kluge and Negt, as well as in theories of Nancy Fraser and Michael Warner, counterpublics are heterogeneous structures—they involve structures as well as spontaneity and they proceed according to critique, although the "experience," as depicted in *Public Sphere and Experience*, allows imagining the critique coming after more emotional acts, not necessarily rooted in rational analysis. This is, I believe, a big step away from the rigidly rationalist ontology of the public sphere presented by Habermas, as well as from Adorno's negative dialectics, featuring reflexive acts of contestation always already mediated by theory. Even though Kluge and Negt are usually classified as rooted in critical theory, their notion of experience actually pushes their work to the borders of that paradigm.

Counterpublics is a transversal notion, seeking the possibility of understanding how heterogeneous and often opposed parts of the social realm still aim at the same political targets and sometimes—as in the case of feminism—manage to succeed regardless of internal conflicts and sharp differences. The notion of the common, far more anti-institutional in the formulation offered by Negri and Hardt, still can be—as Gerald Raunig's work shows—expanded on instituent practices, sometimes growing from within the institutions in crisis. The unintended, mistaken or misfit actions sometimes lead to political changes, yet they usually need to join more institutionalized structures. This is the case in most feminist examples—without institutionalized actions such as court cases, changes in the structures of workplaces and so on, the hashtags would be reducible to a leisure activity online. Yet they are not.

The notion of territory, indicating the possibility of new beginnings in Deleuze and Guattari's *A Thousand Plateaus,* is not marked by heroic masculine figures claiming their rights or fighting for them.[23] They are thus a particularly interesting inspiration for the notion of weak resistance, which also aims to avoid such hegemonic references and tries to find alternatives. The territory starts in a moment of deception and weakness, in confrontation with an overwhelming fear or danger. The opening paragraph of the chapter "Of the Refrain" depicts:

A child in the dark, gripped with fear, comforts himself by singing under his breath. He walks and halts to his song. Lost, he takes shelter, or orients himself with his little song as best as he can. The song is like a rough sketch of a calming and stabilizing, calm and stable, center in the heart of chaos. Perhaps the child skips as he sings, hastens or slows his pace. But the song itself is already a skip:

it jumps from chaos to the beginnings of order in chaos and is in danger of breaking apart at any moment. There is always sonority in Ariadne's thread. Or the song of Orpheus.[24]

The little song the boy depicted by Deleuze and Guattari starts singing marks a transformation, begins a new constellation, a new assemblage. It is not a triumphant anthem of a new nation opposed to a clearly defined enemy. It is a silent tune aimed at survival, not at victory. And yet things unfold in an unprecedented way: "We can never be sure we will be strong enough, for we have no system, only lines and movements."[25]

Deleuze and Guattari built their concept of *ritournelle* in reference to romanticism, the individual reaching out to the other, who is either dead or whose alterity is complete and excludes communication. Yet, the passage in *A Thousand Plateaus* depicting the terrified child, an artist, possibly also a population in despair, seems to also preclude some sort of sublation, overcoming the ultimate solitude in the creation of some new quality, in change, which I dare call historic, although the authors do not, and they themselves seem quite surprised by the somewhat Hegelian sound of the chapter they write.[26] A very important characteristic of territory is that it always produces its deterritorialization: "To produce a deterritorialized refrain as the final end of music, release it in the Cosmos, that is more important than building a new system."[27] Possibly against the intentions of Deleuze and Guattari, who discuss artists and children and not massive social movements in the "Of the Refrain" chapter of *A Thousand Plateaus*, I would like to think of Solidarność in terms of what I will call "making territory." Technical aspects of this seem particularly important both for the making of this particular workers' union and for the territory, depicted as "a direct relation of material forces" and not the relation between form and matter or something similar.[28] The sudden appearance of a new form of politics, a new or subaltern class in the sphere of the visible, or in the public, should not be solely seen as a "war machine" or even an "abstract machine." In the territorial, the historical context shaped by the particular moment of the appearance of a particular assemblage is more clear, allowing us to grasp the specificity of the event without simultaneously emphasizing its exceptionality to the extent of opening metaphysical speculation. The rather poetic suggestion of opening the territory to the cosmos might and perhaps should be read as a suggestion of historical change. Just like the territorial in Deleuze and Guattari's *A Thousand Plateaus*, so too the unexpected appearance of Solidarność in Poland in 1980 at least in part originated as a new beginning in opposition to existing trends. It was organized and assembled from abundance, creativity or curiosity rather than from a reactionary/resentment-based response to the existing order. It was also not entirely a case of a heroic, macho resistance.

A fragment in *A Thousand Plateaus* might be indicative: "In Kafka, it is impossible to separate the erection of a great paranoid bureaucratic machine from the installation of little schizo machines of becoming-dog or becoming-beetle."[29] In order to fully embrace the events of August 1980 in Gdańsk and then in the whole of Poland, we should probably imagine several paranoid bureaucratic machines, such as the state authorities, the police, the Communist Party headquarters (both in Warsaw and in Moscow), the Catholic Church and so on; and millions of schizo machines of becoming "x," where "x" signifies all kinds of new beginnings both on an individual and a group level. Theory cannot believe in innocence or purity and therefore is obliged to be skeptical about the myth of "innocent beginnings," which does not necessarily mean petrified by melancholy or nostalgia. The resistance to one's own innocence, the complex knowledge of complicity, is—particularly in the times of highly competitive, neoliberal academia—an obligation, not just a theoretical choice.

Today we witness the growing popularity of alternatives to the classical, Western, masculine, white, individualist, straight and heroic subject of political agency, where the multitude of ordinary, weak, feminine, queer, trans, Black, ordinary subjects produce historical changes through their differences—but also through their commonality. This is another aspect of the common that I find quite extraordinary, although it was never really emphasized by Negri and Hardt. The common also signals the ordinary and popular, as in the "common folk," "the everyday" or "the rabble." This secondary meaning of the word opens ways to speculate about the deep opposition of their project to that of the exceptional sovereignty depicted by Schmitt.

The revolution of the everyday is in fact the revolution of the ordinary and the common, of the nonheroic and the weak who follow the model of the singing mouse in Franz Kafka's short story "Josephine the Singer, or the Mouse Folk" rather than that of classical heroes. In his account of the protests against the neoliberal transformation of the university, Raunig makes very interesting use of Kafka's singing mouse. He aims at the possibility of a singularity, which is not exceptional, which does not take its political agency and significance from heroic bravery but rather from commonality and sameness with others in the mice folk. The prestigious exceptionality, often earned with heroism and bravery in the male-dominated, patriarchal political model, is thus dissolved by means of ordinary, everyday, somewhat shy agency, which can lead to exceptional results, yet it is not performed as exceptional. Raunig writes: "No pathos emanates from Josephine, no messianic strength, no great notes. The weak event falls short of the strength of the many. And yet the force of attraction of the singular becomes evident, a desire in the entire mouse folk, when even the slightest impression arises that Josephine could sing."[30] The weakness and strength of the common is understood as the making of the *ritournelle*, as the becoming of the refrain in which it is possible to see the other side of the common, its banality and unexceptionality: "It is not a fable and has no linear plot. Instead, it is a treatise on the relation between multitude and singularity, on the form in which singularity emerges from the multitude and how it falls back into the multitude again."[31] Kafka's Josephine, the singing mouse, is perhaps one of many, and perhaps she does not do much, yet still there is a sense of resistance and unheroic agency that emanates from her.

Kafka's mouse sings without knowing it or even choosing it; she thinks she is doing what every other mouse does, but she isn't. Similar to the cyborg in Donna Haraway's *A Cyborg Manifesto*, ordinary resistance does not have an innocent history, does not have a utopian future and does not rely on idealistic claims. The mouse is part of a flat circuit of relations, a member of a heterotopic social space shaped by forces belonging to military complexes or state machines. She is, however, a peculiar figure, for she dismantles the norms of the world in which she lives while just being herself, without making particularly strong claims.

The dynamics between the weak and the strong are very central also in the geopolitical and colonial contest. Postcolonial and decolonial theories provide several ways in which weakness is used strategically. Homi Bhabha, Édouard Glissant and Gloria Anzaldúa are among those who explore the weakness constituted by the unclarity and ambivalence of the colonized. Anzaldúa rejects the obligation to deliver the "straight story" habitually imposed by the colonizers or "la migra": the border guard. For the refugee, there is no straight story to tell. If the question were asked to the white guard, the story would also not be straight, especially if he was not armed and the person asking the question was. The demand of a "straight story" is for Anzaldúa a privilege of the white, Anglo man. From the perspective of this privilege, she and every other woman of color seems contradictory and impure. And she responds: "It's your label that splits me."[32] I explored her work in discussions of racism against Ukrainians, Belarussians and Russians in Poland. But the in-betweenness that concerns her is one of literally "living on the borders" of gender, race, ethnicity, languages, class, sexual identity and so on. Being such a border crosser subverts all distinctions, splits the binary codes. Exactly like the word "Polish": not yet Western, but not exactly from the East, not peripheral, but there are peripheries, as "Polish" definitely means "from the core." The deconstructive principle, which Derrida locates in the very word *perestroika*, emblematic of the East European transition of 1989, is one that dismantles both order and, at the same time, the neoliberal order's most persuasive arm.[33] The deconstruction is never chaotic or accidental. It also supports structures of power. Slavoj Žižek depicted the Balkans as the phantasmatic "other" of the West—the anarchistic aspects of the ethnic groups inhabiting the "former Yugoslavia" should, in his perspective, be seen as a formative part of the "former West's" supposed "order."[34]

Several other authors from Eastern Europe use postcolonial theories in a comparative context to make sense of the Soviet presence in their countries. Politically this has particularly strong anticommunist consequences, like in the work of Mykola Riabczuk concerning Ukraine.[35] For others the postcolonial references are necessary to depict Central Europe as a space in-between. Maria Janion analyzes Polish history as one of a double experience of being colonized and colonizing, in the process of Christianization (around the year 1000, Christianity came to Poland, first in a conquest and then as a more peaceful process, and it spread in the later centuries to the East) and industrialization.[36] This analysis emphasizes the particularly perplexed routes of colonial processes, therefore shifting the usually linear postcolonial critique into a more rhizomatic one. And these approaches seem especially inspiring and similar to the tasks of my own project. The connection between postcolonial theory or, more generally, the history of colonization and the postsocialist or former East still seems extravagant or new. An article from 2001 is widely quoted as a groundbreaking new proposal for making this connection.[37] There are certainly some new aspects to discover in this exchange, and it is true that it has only really been explored in the last two decades. Nevertheless, there are theories and entire paradigms that draw large-scale comparisons between the history of colonization and the development of Eastern Europe, and there also exist direct encounters between individual representatives of these otherwise distant locations and contexts.

In the 1950s and 1960s, Warsaw-based scholars Witold Kula and Marian Małowist developed comparative studies of the development of South America and Eastern Europe as dependent on the West and kept in the dependency. The key elements of the feudal system were preserved there much longer than in the West. This blocked the development of industrial capitalism and/or constituted these regions of the world as the supplementary resources for the West.[38] Their theory of dependency was later continued by Immanuel Wallerstein in his world systems theory, within which the aforementioned concept of semi-periphery was coined around 1975.[39] In Wallerstein's view, semi-peripheries try to become part of the global core, make all efforts not to be seen as periphery and are kept in the in-between position, constantly lured with promises of joining the center soon, but these are never fully realized. Although Poland was already enumerated as semi-periphery in Wallerstein's article, it became an even more appropriate description after 1989.[40]

From its beginnings, the concept of "semi-periphery" signified a double function: that of being colonized and colonizing; dependent and forcing others into dependency. It actually captures the majority of contemporary states struggling between development and/or crisis and marginalization. In world systems theory, semi-peripheries are situated between core countries and peripheries, between the zones of "concentrated high-profit, high-wage and high technology diversified production" and spaces of "concentrated low-profit, low-technology, low-wage."[41] Wallerstein argues that semi-peripheries act like peripheries to core countries and like central countries to peripheral ones; they are also capable of taking more advantage from global economic crises than the two other kinds of countries. Wallerstein emphasizes that "in moments of world economic downturn, semi-peripheral countries can usually expand control of their home market at the expense of core producers, and expand their access to neighbouring peripheral markets, again at the expense of core producers."[42] He also explains how semi-peripheral countries, which are often successful in transforming an economic crisis for their gain, need to appropriate the gains of other semi-peripheries to their advantage. Wallerstein's approach encapsulates the realities of this scheme very poignantly, when he states: "This is simply the state-level adaptation of the traditional 'dog eat dog' workings of capitalism. This is not 'development' but successful expropriation of world surplus."[43]

There is something inappropriate and weak about the semi-periphery. Not only is it neither center nor periphery, but it is also both of them. Eastern Europe tends to define itself in reference. As there is the decolonial for the colonized, there does not seem to be a non-dialectical position for places such as Poland. But on the other hand, it always introduces some sort of doubt and dissonance; it is always "like as if" or "almost," always in-between. This in-betweenness, a form of mediation but also a form of liquidation of any sort of purity, involves destabilization and chaos.

The colonial and postcolonial system of dependencies was also explored in iconic feminist Maria Janion's theories of Polish literature. In her work *Uncanny Slavdom*, she portrays the cultural history of Poland since its embrace of Christianity from the West in the year 996 as a culture of in-betweeness, based on contradictions between the East-West, Christian-pagan, industrial/natural and so on.[44] Similarly to Kula and Małowist, she juxtaposes the Western linear, "clear" development history with that of Poland, which has counterpoints and detours. In her perspective, the fundamental ambivalence of Polish culture allowed its ethnic and cultural heterogeneity, but it also provided effective ground for identitarian panic and the violence issuing from it. Her argument found some interesting development in a public letter she wrote to the organizers of the Congress of Polish Culture in fall 2016, where she demanded an end to the "heroic messianism" and all the martyrdom it brings. A more ordinary, everyday politics should begin in Poland.[45] This statement, contextualized in the feminist protests of 2016 supports my own search for weak resistance and the nonheroic forms of political agency. It also constitutes a sharp and inspiring response to the constant search for heroism practiced by recent Polish governments.

Weakness is a particularly important element of contemporary avant-gardes, particularly in feminist art. It can obviously be discussed as a "sublation" of the very idea of the avant-garde, yet I believe this sublation perpetuates certain important factors. The rejection of the notion of the avant-garde, recurring in the contemporary European context, where artists demand common participation in art, fulfills the biggest hopes of the early twentieth-century avant-garde, that of doing away with the art/life distinction in particular. According to Boris Groys, it is precisely the democratizing power of the avant-garde art that makes it weak, as in weak universalism.[46] Following artists from East and West, Groys suggests that a weak messianic force has manifested itself in twentieth-century avant-garde art, determining its democratic force, on the one hand, and leading to rejection by the public, on the other. What for him stands as the genderless, classless paradox of a subject formation deprived of any historical and cultural specificity, for me has only been made possible by particular, embodied and socially specific articulations of art, its makers, critics, audience and/or participants, such as feminist artists like Zorka Wollny, whose work I discussed earlier, or Ewa Partum.[47]

In contrast to Hal Foster, Groys defines the avant-garde as a practice that proceeds as a version of "weak universalism" in its inclusiveness and tendency to abstraction, resulting in extremely accessible forms. For him, avant-garde artworks are distant reminders of Walter Benjamin's "weak messianism," with their weakening of signs, the de-professionalization of art and reductions. What is missing in Groys's analysis, though, is an assessment of the materiality of art, on the one hand, and of its makers and/or participants, on the other. Idealist theories of culture, art in particular, pretending that artists' embodied experiences do not inform their practice should be replaced with an understanding of art as a materialized, historicized practice of particular people in a particular time, using a particular technology and mindset. This was clear for Benjamin; it should also be clear now. Yet in Groys's narrative, the political involvement of artists is ignored, the deep evolution of the means of their production is neglected, the massive appearance of women and other hitherto excluded groups in the field of art is missing. All the aspects in which the materiality of art transforms, resulting in its subsequent successful deheroicization and dehomogenization, are not considered, resulting in the making of yet another art theory that moves freely above the embodied labor of art's producers. Regardless of these flaws, Groys's essay offers a visionary concept of "weak universalism" and particularly inspiring insight into the prospects of reading the historical avant-gardes beyond a heroic, sexist perspective.

In the examples of weak resistance and references discussed previously, the resignation from the classical, masculine and heroic model of political agency is very clear. Theoretical contexts of these examples are very different; however, each of them entails the rejection of domination and strength, at least strategically—in Havel's "powerless," Deleuze and Guattari's "territorialization," in the semi-peripheral and colonized, as depicted by Wallerstein, Anzaldúa and others, it is always the weak that come forth. And with it also come the characteristics usually attributed to the "other" of the white, Western, masculine, straight and privileged—the mundane, ordinary and everyday common forms of resistance, which in some cases merely means persistence and survival, although what it brings about is often subversion, rejection and transformation of the existing norm. We are so used to the brave, heroic model of political agency that these forms of resistance have been kept invisible or marginalized until recently, when in different academic and activist fields these strategies became interesting or even central. Some of these examples were discussed here. Social movements, protests and mobilizations, as well as theorists, reclaim the necessity of overcoming the heroic, patriarchal and exceptional modes of agency. The notion of weak resistance provides such opportunity, allowing us to explain the political agency of the counterpublics of the common. It also helps to imagine the antifascist future.

These excursions to the not-so-distant past cannot exclude places and events that have been depicted as failed. We cannot only learn from Weimar, Paris and San Francisco. Gdańsk, Malaysia, Kiyv, Cairo, Istanbul or Calcutta, and so many other places, have hosted resistance movements from which we can learn. The geopolitics of location definitely needs to decentralize in order for our models of political resistance not to repeat the oppressive hegemony of the colonial past. I think that with the impurity and in-betweenness typical of semi-peripheries, with state communist as well as neoliberal pasts and their past and contemporary feminist movements, this region, and the Polish cases more specifically, clearly demonstrate how such classical models of politics as Habermas's "public sphere" require critique and replacement—not solely because their authors are not Marxist enough, but because they contain such exclusive presumptions as the "private/public divide," which artificially cuts our lived experiences into those who can and those who cannot be political, despite a world where everything can be a political matter.

Conclusion:
Toward Antifascist Futures

In the previous four chapters of this book, I have discussed several large-scale social mobilizations, operating as counterpublics of the common, as well as some of their constraints, particularly those issued by the conservative vision of political agency, and those resulting from the more general context of communicative capitalism, which is a notion of Jodi Dean, whose work I sometimes disagree with. There is another focus of this book, expressed particularly in the last chapter—that of weak resistance, which is partly inspired by the counterpublics discussed here, and partly constructed following the work of Benjamin, Havel, Halberstam and other authors. In the early Solidarność, as well as in the recent feminist protests in Poland and globally (#BlackProtest, the Women's Strike, #MeToo and other campaigns), I see great examples of counterpublics, as depicted by Nancy Fraser, in their disagreement with current governments, as well as with the cultural hegemony of the conservative exclusion of those excluded and marginalized—women, workers, the proletariat and the colonized. Their modes of organizing, as well as their claims, have many similarities with the common discussed in the books of Antonio Negri and Michael Hardt, particularly in their being formed in struggle, according to the mobilized affects of the multitude, and in their search for overcoming the public/private divide by means of a third option—that of experienced, embodied and contextualized collective agency. It is this confrontation with the public/private divide that the common and the counterpublics are most similar, thus this is the central element in my effort to think about them together, as "counterpublics of the common."

The scale of the mobilizations discussed here is not accidental. In various forms of political activism, we see a preoccupation with the small scale and local actions. This focus on small structures has already been criticized by various theorists as insufficient in the current state of global ecological catastrophe, as well as in the politics of the state of exception that has been introduced in multiple forms by fascist politicians and informal groups around the globe. In such a moment, as Patricia Reed and other theorists rightly remind us, scale matters; however, I believe there is a different mode of embracing this rather than by smashing small-scale initiatives, as Žižek very persuasively does in his sometimes quite fantastic critiques concerning, for instance, charity or small changes in lifestyle, which for him only perpetuate capitalism. Such practices resemble the Catholic ritual of confession—we pledge our guilt and receive absolution, and we can sin further, which in this case usually means that we do not challenge capitalism at its core. It is clear that the time of hegemony of small-scale avant-garde and exclusive groups is over, however—as they can be, and often actually are, small laboratories of new political agency, they should be considered precisely as such and not as the only solution for the global problems, which they definitely cannot solve without larger-scale movements.

There is a pressing need for a popular front against fascism. As Negri and Hardt rightly argue, it cannot only be a reactive move, solely opposing various revitalizations of the fascist doctrine. We also need to imagine and rehearse alternatives, to check whether "another world is possible," as the great alterglobalization slogan dictated. As I tried to signal in this book, our political organizations as well as our theories need to embrace the weaknesses of particular humans and nonhumans, as well as groups. The focus on failure is not meant to exclude effective actions or to merely celebrate collapses. It is—and here I follow Rosa Luxemburg—strategic, as a response to the necessary, yet never final, failures of the effort to move beyond imperial capitalism.

The future forms of political organization, be it counterpublics of the common or otherwise, also need to embrace the very basic human need of solidarity, a sense of acting in common and belonging, which has been deeply altered by precarizing processes, pushing many into instability that ruins any prospect of radical political action. Such a sense is still vibrant in public gatherings and demonstrations, where participants understand, again, that—contrary to Margaret Thatcher's infamous statement—there is such thing as society, and sometimes it can go against the alienated preoccupation with profit. The notion of the public, rooted in such a sense of togetherness, is combined with the critical, oppositional vector of agency in the notion and practice of counterpublics. However, the affective substance of such agency belongs to the common, and thus one cannot move without the other.

Our experience of fulfillment, often expressed in the positive memories of particularly "good demonstrations," is not only present because of the nice banners or great numbers of participants; this would be a spectacular reading of such events. It feels good to be there because of the profound, sometimes touching feeling of sharing the same claims with so many others. Here, the effect of scale is not merely a media scandal; it is also and above all rooting us in the "we, the people" sense of acting together. This sense of togetherness and shared purposes and critiques further fuels the conviction toward changing the sometimes unbearable status quo. This depiction of the feelings and actions of the common can of course be seen as a fetishi-zation of the collective voice, yet if this is a common in revolt—if it is therefore a counterpublic of the common—we are probably witness-ing a transformation of the existing world into a new entity, even if in a small aspect or particular dimension. Yet as Sibylle Peters argues in "On Becoming Many", this perhaps is the only way to rehearse the "being common" in its critiques of general inequality and its particu-lar form, as many times as is necessary to transform society and introduce new politics into it.[1]

Some argue against such optimistic vision of the collective affect. In *The Cultural Politics of Emotion*, Sara Ahmed sharply details how nationalist, radical right-wing movements are fueled by love.[2] She discusses the love for sameness as a condition of possibility in the hatred demonstrated against the "others" in contemporary Western societies. These pointed images cannot, however, erase the needs of belonging, solidarity and togetherness from the progressive picture of political agency. It is not the necessary logical conclusion that since there is love at the core of fascist mobilization, solidarity cannot be an affect uniting the left. The narrative offered by Ahmed is backed up by Žižek's psychoanalytic critique, which, in his discussion of the Balkans, also presents certain restrictions in his endorsement of affect on the left.[3]

Yet the common also feels. Should the theory and practice of the counterpublics of the common resign from affect and embrace the solely rationalist paradigm so typical of the left? Let me recall a letter Karl Marx wrote to Ludwig Feuerbach, when they were still on speaking terms, in August 1844:

> These Berliners do not regard themselves as *men* who *criticize*, but as *critics* who, *incidentally*, have the misfortune of being men . . . This criticism therefore lapses into a sad and supercilious intellectualism. *Consciousness or self-consciousness* is regarded as the *only* human quality. Love, for example, is rejected, because the loved one is only an "*object.*" Down with the object. It is therefore regarded as the greatest crime if the critic displays *feeling* or *passion*, he must be an *ironical ice-cold* [Sage].[4]

I am not claiming that affect will solve our issues, but I also do not want to subscribe to a critique that contradicts an important part of the lived experience and thus fails to build a theory of the public, which we so badly need.

The affective should be recognized not solely as an aspect of the largely ignored field of reproductive labor. While this recognition is correct, it is insufficient for our understanding of the public and political agency. In order to build the theory and practice of counterpublics of the common, we need to embrace involvement in the political, which is also affective. Wilhelm Reich argued that the masses do not "choose" fascism, they desire it. The implications of his insistence on the desiring practice of the social realm can be found in Deleuze and Guattari, who acknowledge the importance of Reich's observation in their *Anti-Oedipus,* but also in Kluge and Negt's *Public Sphere and Experience,* where they reference Reich in order to define their vision of the lived experience. In Negri and Hardt's work, the multitude, the common and the counterpowers, which they discuss in each of their books, are always affective. There seems, therefore, to be no contradiction between the counterpublics and the common on the level of understanding affect as part of the political.

Counterpublics of the common share the antifascist orientation. In Kluge and Negt's work, it is explicit (as it was in Habermas, regardless of the problems with his liberal perspective). In the works of Hardt and Negri, the common is not only anti-neoliberal, but also anti-authoritarian. Thus, the general antifascist line seems obvious. However, one more thing has to be acknowledged if the theory and practice of antifascism is to be contemporary and not merely historical: feminism and the centrality of women's rights must sit at the core of our understanding of the contemporary state of exception. The *homo sacer*, the contemporary subject of oppression, is gendered. There is no returning to the "universal subject" of the West. We are different, and the assaults on our integrity, safety and dignity vary depending on gender, race, social and economic status, sexuality and geopolitics, still cutting the world into the colonizing and the colonized, even though this happens in convoluted ways, since peripheries open up in the suburbs and centers of many metropolitan cities in Europe, while the center more and more often appears in the former peripheries.

The centrality of women's issues and reproductive rights and labor in contemporary feminist movements allows a focus on particular, embodied experiences as those building the lived experience of the common. These issues also transversally cut through contemporary societies, building counterpublics across class, race and other divisions. Such contingent universality, which can be claimed and used strategically and should never be essentialized, is one of the new aspects of contemporary feminist counterpublics of the common. By their composition, they allow understanding and resistance to other forms of oppression: those appearing in the labor market, those caused by war, colonial practices and racism. Thus they resist fascism even if their declared topics might seem more specific or limited.

Given today's rise of fascist politics, resistance might seem futile, yet it is necessary. It cannot be maintained as simply the agency of the privileged classes, genders and ethnic groups; it cannot only be perceived as the politics of the West. There are so many places where the counterpublics of the common are created that instead of erasing them by our traditional habits, we should perhaps learn how to understand them as a global trend, in their diversity and heterogeneity.

This book attempts to build an antifacist theory and politics for today, one in which the core is feminist. Weak resistance and counterpublics of the common both have a serious feminist accent in the book's method, purposes and inspirations; they undermine the hegemony of heroic agency rooted in the colonial, Western, masculinist subject to instead prioritize minoritarian positions and perspectives. This is not a refusal of the large-scale or a declaration of melancholic resignation. The narrative offered in this book follows the resistance movements in present and past Poland as well as globally while avoiding "easy fix" kinds of solutions. Yes, the process of large-scale counterpublics is one of many failures and weaknesses; however, it is also one of hope, solidarity and sometimes social and political change.

We are perhaps closer than we think to a major transformation of the core ideas of the subject, politics and resistance. Individualism is shrinking, not solely because of right-wing populism but also due to the dismantling of masculinist, white, straight and privileged subjectivities in historical and theoretical processes around the globe. The recent developments of Marxist ideas in various fields of theory and politics, as well as the recent mass access to feminism, proceed transversally in all layers of different societies and fuel the political imagination. The feminist strategies in Rojava, the Black Protests and Women's Strike in Poland and those in South Korea, Italy, Mexico, Argentina and the United States, as well as the International Women's Strike, together with #MeToo and similar campaigns, show how this wave of feminist politics suddenly appears against the fascist tide. This unprecedented, international and egalitarian "fifth wave" of feminism should not be reduced to a mere "addition" to progressive politics today. It is the core of contemporary antifascism and should be seen as such.

Today the main principle of liberal individualism is under attack from several different positions. Within the critical Marxist tradition, the privilege of bourgeois, Western individualism and the very concept of political subjectivity have been revised by such authors as Kluge and Negt, Raunig and Lorey. Operaist Marxism, along with Hardt and Negri, Bifo and others, argues for a discussion of the common as a counterpower. Feminist theorists as diverse as Fraser, Honig, Haraway and Federici build feminist politics of alliances in solidarity, in which heterogeneity is not merely a liberal principle of fetishized difference, but it becomes a powerful element of dismantling the heroic vision of political agency in which the brave, Wertherian hero acts against all and wins. In theories of counterpublics, sororal pacts or other versions of feminist politics aim beyond appreciation of the status quo, still proudly presented by liberal feminism as the main goal. Failure is understood as part of the historical process. There is something deeply Hegelian in this transition of progressive politics beyond the horizon of triumphant victory. This sudden realization—that within the historical process the small, weak and oppressed find ways of gaining recognition and transforming history—means that there is a need to revisit the individualist and heroic principles of today's still largely masculinist Marxist politics and instead bring in some feminism. Not liberal feminism, which pretends that acting as brave men provides women's victory, but feminism ready to revise the core principles of neoliberal individualism.

As Hardt and Negri rightly point out, our current disputes regarding the old "reformism or revolution" question are outdated. We need to create new visions of revolution and reform, and perhaps we need to completely revise this division. The transversal principle I focused on seems to force us to rethink radicalism compared to former generations. The beginnings of Solidarność show how the same event can at once be a reform and a revolution, a moderate transition and a major change at the same time. Even today's lawyers cannot decide, after some forty years of discussion, whether it was a revolution or reform.[5] This clearly means that new forms of theory and action are already on their way, and we need to embrace them as well as keep our critical apparatus ready.

Seen from this perspective, the feminist movements, mobilizations and protests, as well as the juridical and institutional mechanisms of gender equality, and such campaigns as #MeToo allow for imagining new politics and new assemblages. These counterpublics of the common should be seen as a response to the neoliberal model of capitalism, in which—as we learn from Lisa Duggan, the conservative pseudo-care always accompanies austerity cuts.[6] They are not merely a "left-wing populism," since the transversal method combines popular claims and participation with intellectual and artistic work, including theory. Therefore, while not rejecting the concept of left-wing populism but actually embracing it, I would prefer to think of counterpublics of the common as those built across class and embracing heterogeneity and plurality in expressed demands, positions and perspectives without resigning from the large scale.

The current rise of fascism demands answers. Offering an answer and resisting does not merely mean being incapable of seeing the possibly dark future. It actually allows seeing the future as one dialectically forming in the historical process, transversally combining visions, movements, political theories and practice. Visions of the future need not be invented; they are born in social struggles, and our visions can participate in their making but we cannot fully schedule these swells. While focusing on the future, we need to stop pretending that we can "invent the future." We are parts of social processes, and thus our agency for the future is merely participatory. This togetherness, however, and the ability to conceptualize and enact it without resignation, resentment or repression, can be the future's greatest asset. Let's try not to ruin it with a false sense of individual agency.

This book would never have happened without many people and groups acting and thinking against fascism in the last decades. It was written of a sense of responsibility—that certain things, such as sexism, colonialism and class privilege, should be stopped, and certain other things, including fascism, should never happen again. It is a tribute to all those who consecrated their lives and futures for us to use the opportunities we have to continue their struggle and expand the possibilities of egalitarian politics. Perhaps it will not disappoint them.

Acknowledgements

This book would never have happened if it wasn't for countless people and institutions; there is no way for me to enumerate them all. I would like to thank Tariq Ali and Rosie Warren for their kind collaboration at Verso and Marsha Bradfield for her generous editing of the early version of this text. I would like to thank my friends and colleagues: Katarzyna Kasia and Ninka, Agata Lisiak, Ela Korolczuk, Ola Karasińska, Aleka Polisiewicz, Zorka Wollny, Justyna Jaworska, Julia Junosza-Szaniawska and Lolo, Gyrcia, Małgosia Kozera, Janek, Sylwia Urbańska, Mateusz Janik, Mikołaj Ratajczak, Anna Nacher, Monika Royowska-Stangret, Beata Kowalska, Góska Myk, Stefan Zgliczyński, Jacek Kołtan, Andrzej Leśniak, Joanna Warsza, Darek Szendel, Natalia Romik, Basia Godlewska-Bujok, Joanna Figiel, Oliver Bauerhenn and Armando, Patricia Reed, Daniel Muzyczuk, Aga Pindera, Alexandro Facchini and Ola for supporting me in various ways during the process of writing and researching this book. A special thank you should be directed to Martha Rosler, Gerald Raunig, Judith Revel and Antonio Negri for being great public intellectuals.

I would like to thank the students and friendly colleagues in my department at the University of Warsaw for their support and solidarity. A particular thank you goes to the students and colleagues who supported me and other colleagues in 2012 during the restructuring of our department at Jagiellonian University (Katedra Kultury Współczesnej). Seeing a strike action initiated by the students, who demanded the immediate end of the problematic transformation of the university into a neoliberal factory and supported their professors, was the biggest surprise and inspiration I've ever experienced.

Scholars at various institutes where I have conducted my research and work in the last fifteen years were particularly supportive and inspiring. This includes, in particular: Paola Bacchetta at the BBRG, University of California, Berkeley; Cornelia Klinger at the IWM in Vienna; Christopher Holzhey, Manuele Gragnolati and Claudia Peppel at the ICI Berlin; Elżbieta Matynia at the New School in New York; Anna Jonasdottir at the University of Orebro; Jerzy Kochan at the University of Szczecin; Małgorzata Radkiewicz, Beata Kowalska at Jagiellonian University in Kraków; Magdalena Środa; Piotr Laskowski; late professors Marek Siemek and Aleksander Ochocki and the librarians at the University of Warsaw; and Andrzej Leder at the Polish Academy of Science in Warsaw. I would also like to thank all my colleagues and students in the aforementioned institutions.

My parents are also responsible for some content in this book—as an activist, a politician and a scholar, my father, Dr. Henryk Majewski, definitely shaped important parts of my way of combining scholarly work and activism, and as an artist, my mother, Magdalena Majewska-Keane, was a feminist before any of us knew the word. Her husband, John Keane, was also very patient and supportive, so a thank you note is very much in place.

I would also like to thank the brave people in contemporary feminist movements for constant inspiration and struggle. While I am truly grateful to all the friends, colleagues and family mentioned above, and also those whom I forgot to mention, I am the only person responsible for this book's weaknesses.

Bibliography

Adorno, Theodor W. and Max Horkheimer. *Dialectic of Enlightenment*, transl. E. Jephcott, Stanford: Stanford University Press, 2002.

Agamben, Giorgio. *State of Exception*, transl. K. Attell, Chicago: University of Chicago Press, 2005.

Ahmed, Sara. *Willful Subjects*, Durham: Duke University Press, 2014.

____. *The Cultural Politics of Emotion*, New York: Routledge, 2004.

Ali, Tariq. *The Radical Center*, London: Verso, 2015.

____. "Between Past and Future," *New Left Review* 80 (April–March), 2013.

Anzaldúa, Gloria. *Borderlands/ La Frontera*, San Francisco: Aunt Lute Books, 1987.

Baczko, Bronisław. *Wyobrażenia społeczne. Szkice o nadziei i pamięci zbiorowej*, Warszawa: PWN, 1994.

Baudrillard, Jean. *The Gulf War Did Not Take Place*, Bloomington: Indiana University Press, 1995.

____. "No Pity for Sarajevo"; "The West's Serbianization"; "When the West Stands In for the Dead," in T. Cushman and S. G. Meštrović (eds.), *This Time We Knew: Western Responses to Genocide in Bosnia*, New York: NYU Press, 1996.

Bayat, Asaf. "Revolution in Bad Times," *New Left Review* 80 (April–March), 2013.

Benjamin, Walter. *Selected Writings*, transl. E. Jephcott, vol. 1, Cambridge: Harvard University Press, 1996.

____. *Selected Writings*, transl. E. Jephcott, vol. 4, Cambridge: Harvard University Press, 2003.

Berlant, Lauren. *Cruel Optimism*, Durham: Duke University Press, 2011.

____. "The Subject of True Feeling," in A. Sarat and T. Kearn (eds.), *Cultural Pluralism, Identity Politics, and the Law*, Ann Arbor: University of Michigan Press, 1999.

Bey, Hakim. *Temporary Autonomous Zone*, New York: Autonomedia, 1991.

Bhattacharia, Tithi. "Socializing Security, Unionizing Work," in *Where Freedom Starts: Sex, Power, Violence, #Metoo*, London: Verso, 2017.

____. "Mapping Social Reproduction Theory," published February 15, 2018, Versobooks.com.

Bloch, Ernst. *The Utopian Function of Art and Literature: Selected Essays*, transl. J. Zipes and F. Mecklenberg, Cambridge: MIT Press, 1988.

Buden, Boris. *Strefa przejścia. O końcu postkomunizmu*, Warszawa: Wydawnictwo Krytyki Politycznej, 2012.

Butler, Judith. *Gender Trouble: Feminism and the Subversion of Identity*, New York: Routledge, 1990.

____. *Notes Toward a Performative Theory of the Assembly*, Harvard: Harvard University Press, 2015.Butler, Judith and Gayatri Chakravorty Spivak, *Who Sings the Nation State: Language, Politics, Belonging*, London: Seagull, 2011.

Calhoun, Craig (ed.), *Habermas and the Public Sphere*, Cambridge: MIT Press, 1992.

Cixous, Hélène. "The Laugh of the Medusa," transl. K. Cohen, P. Cohen, *Signs: Journal of Women in Culture and Society* 1: 4, 1976.

____. "Od *Śmiechu Meduzy* do rynku wojny. An Interview," *Lewą Nogą* 16, 2004.

Dalla Costa, Mariarosa and Selma James. *Women and the Subversion of the Community/A Woman's Place*, London: Butler and Tanner Ltd., 1972.

Danius, Sara, Stefan Jonsson and Gayatri Chakravorty Spivak. "An Interview with Gayatri Chakravorty Spivak," *boundary* 2, 20: 2, 1993.

Davis, Angela, Gayatri Chakravorty Spivak and Nikita Dhawan. "Planetary Utopias," *Radical Philosophy* 2: 5, 2019.

Dean, Jodi. "Why the Net is Not a Public Sphere," *Constellations* 10: 1, 2003.Dean, Jodi and Paul Passavant. *The Empire's New Clothes*, New York: Routledge, 2004.

Debord, Guy. *The Society of the Spectacle*, transl. D. Nicholson-Smith, New York: Zone Books, 1994.

Deleuze, Gilles. "Cours Vincennes: Sur la Musique," March 8, 1977, webdeleuze.com.

Deleuze, Gilles and Félix Guattari. *Mille Plateaux*, Paris: Editions du Minuit, 1981.

Derrida, Jacques. *Specters of Marx*, London: Routledge, 1993.

Deutsche, Rosalyn. "Art and Public Space: Questions of Democracy," *Social Text* 33, 1992.

Douglas, Mary. *How Institutions Think*, New York: Syracuse University Press, 1986.

Duggan, Lisa. *The Twilight of Equality? Neoliberalism, Cultural Politics, and the Attack on Democracy*, New York: Beacon Press, 2004.

Dunn, Elizabeth C. *Privatizing Poland: Baby Food, Big Business, and the Remaking of Labor*, New York: Cornell University Press, 2004.

Dzido, Marta. *Kobiety Solidarności*, Warszawa: Świat Książki, 2016.

Fantone, Laura. "Precarious Changes: Gender and Generational Politics in Contemporary Italy," *Feminist Review* 87, 2007.

Federici, Silvia. *Caliban and the Witch*, New York: Autonomedia, 2004.

____. "Precarious Labor: A Feminist Viewpoint," *Journal of Aesthetics and Protest* 1-9: 9, 2008.

Folbre, Nancy. *The Invisible Heart: Economics and Family Values*, New York: New Press, 2001.

Foucault, Michel. "Of Other Spaces: Utopias and Heterotopias," transl. J. Miskowiec, *Architecture, Mouvement, Continuité* 15, 1984.

Fraser, Nancy. "Rethinking the Public Sphere: A Contribution to the Critique of Actually Existing Democracy," *Social Text* 25/26, 1990.

____. "How Feminism Became Capitalism's Handmaiden and How to Reclaim It," *Guardian*, October 14, 2013.

Friszke, Andrzej. *Opozycja polityczna w PRL 1945-1980*, London: Wydawnictwo Aneks, 1994.

____. *Przystosowanie i opór. Studia z dziejów PRL*, Warszawa: Towarzystwo "Więź," 2007.

____. (ed.), *Solidarność 1980-81 od wewnątrz*, Warszawa: Wydawnictwo IPN, 2013.

Garcia, Sandra E. "The Woman Who Created #MeToo Long Before Hashtags," *New York Times*, October 20, 2017.

Garton Ash, Timothy. *The Polish Revolution: Solidarity*, London: Granta Books and Penguin, 1991.

Geremek, Bronisław. *The Margins of Society in Late Medieval Paris*, Cambridge: Cambridge University Press, 2006.

Graff, Agnieszka and Elżbieta Korolczuk, "Gender as "Ebola from Brussels'": The Anti-colonial Frame and the Rise of Illiberal Populism," *Signs: Journal of Women in Culture and Society* 43: 4, 2018.

Groys, Boris. "Weak Universalism," *The e-flux Journal* 15, 2010.

Guattari, Félix. *The Three Ecologies*, transl. I. Pindar and P. Sutton, London and Brunschwick: Athlone Press, 2000.

Habermas, Jurgen. *The Structural Transformation of the Public Sphere: An Inquiry into a Category of Bourgeois Society*, transl. T. Burger, Cambridge: MIT Press, 1989.

____. "The Public Sphere: An Encyclopedia Article," *New German Critique* 3, 1974 [1964].

Halberstam, Judith J. *The Queer Art of Failure*, Durham: Duke University Press, 2010.

Hall, Stuart. "Encoding, Decoding," in S. During (ed.), *The Media Studies Reader*, New York: Routledge, 1993.

Haraway, Donna. *Staying with the Trouble: Making Kin in the Chthulucene*, Durham: Duke University Press, 2016.

____. *Simians, Cyborgs and Women: The Reinvention of Nature*, New York: Routledge, 1991.

____. "Situated Knowledges: The Science Question in Feminism and the Privilege of Partial Perspective," *Feminist Studies* 3: 14, 1988.

Hardt, Michael and Antonio Negri. *Assembly*, Oxford: Oxford University Press, 2017.

____. *Commonwealth*, Cambridge: MIT University Press, 2009.

____. *Empire*, Cambridge: Harvard University Press, 2000.

____. *Multitudes: War and Democracy in the Age of Empire*, New York: Penguin Press, 2004.

Havel, Václav. "The Power of the Powerless," *International Journal of Politics*, 15: 3/4, 1985–6.

Herman, Judith. *Trauma and Recovery: The Aftermath of Violence—from Domestic Abuse to Political Terror*, Basic Books, 1992.

Hill, Mike and Warren Montag (eds.). *Masses, Classes and the Public Sphere*, New York: Verso, 2000.

Holzer, Jerzy. *Solidarność 1980–81: Geneza i historia*, Warszawa: Wydawnictwo Krąg, 1984.

Honig, Bonnie. *Antigone, Interrupted,* Cambridge: Cambridge University Press, 2013.

Honneth, Axel. *The Struggle for Recognition*, Cambridge: MIT Press, 1996.

hooks, bell. *Feminist Theory: From Margin to Center,* London: Pluto Press, 2000.

IPN National Institute of Remembrance. Documentation of the strikes in 1970/71. grudzien70.ipn.gov.pl.

Jameson, Fredric. "On Negt and Kluge," *October* 46, 1988.

Janion, Maria. *Niesamowita słowiańszczyzna,* Kraków: Wydawnictwo Literackie, 2006.

_____. "List do Uczestników Kongresu Kultury Polskiej," 2016, tvn24.com.

Jaworska, Justyna. "*Moda żałobna przed wybuchem powstania styczniowego,*" *Przegląd Humanistyczny 57*: 1(436), 2013.

Jónasdóttir, Anna. *Love Power and Political Interests,* Örebro: Örebro University Press, 1991.

Khatib, Sami. "The Messianic Without Messianism: Walter Benjamin's Materialist Theology," *Anthropology and Materialism* 1, 2013.

Klein, Naomi. *No Logo: Taking Aim at the Brand Bullies,* London: Picador and Random House, 1999.

Kluge, Alexander and Oskar Negt. *Public Sphere and Experience: Analysis of the Bourgeois and Proletarian Public Sphere,* transl. P. Labanyi et al., London: Verso, 2016.

_____. *History and Obstinacy,* transl. R. Langston et al., New York: Zone Books, 2014.

Kondratowicz, Ewa. *Szminka na sztandarze. Kobiety Solidarności 1980–1989,* Warszawa: Wydawnictwo Sic!, 2001.

Korolczuk, Elżbieta. "'The War on Gender' from a Transnational Perspective—Lessons for Feminist Strategising," 2017, pl.boell.org.

Kowalewski, Zbigniew. *Rendez-nous nos usines!: Solidarnosc dans le combat pour l'autogestion ouvrière,* Montreuil: Presse Éd. Communication, 1985.

Kowalski, Sergiusz. *Krytyka solidarnościowego rozumu,* Warszawa: Wydawnictwa Akademickie i Profesjonalne, 2009.

Kubisa, Julia. *Bunt białych czepków*, Warszawa: Wydawnictwo Naukowe Scholar, 2014.

Kuisz, Jarosław. *Charakter prawny Porozumień Sierpniowych 1980–81*, Warszawa: Wydawnictwo TRIO, 2009.

Kusiak, Joanna. "Legal Technologies of Primitive Accumulation: Judicial Robbery and Dispossession-by-Restitution in Warsaw," *International Journal of Urban and Regional Research* 43: 4, 2019.

Laba, Roman. *The Roots of Solidarity: A Political Sociology of Poland's Working Class Democratization*, Princeton: Princeton University Press, 1991.

Lacan, Jacques. *Le séminaire de Jacques Lacan: Livre XX , Encore (1972–1973)*. Paris: Editions du Seuil, 1999.

Laboria Cuboniks. *The Xenofeminist Manifesto*, London: Verso, 2018.

Lipton, Briony. "Gender and Precarity: A Response to Simon During," *Australian Humanities Review* 58, 2015.

Lefebvre, Henri. "The Right to the City," in E. Kofman and E. Lebas (eds.), *Writings on Cities*, Cambridge: Wiley-Blackwell, 1996.

Lopez, Kimberly J., Meghan L. Muldoon and Janet K.L. McKeown. "One Day of #Feminism: Twitter as a Complex Digital Arena for Wielding, Shielding, and Trolling Talk on Feminism," *Leisure Sciences: An Interdisciplinary Journal* 41: 4, 2018.

Lorey, Isabell. *State of Insecurity: Government of the Precarious*, transl. Aileen Derieg, London: Verso, 2015.

Magala, Sławomir (S. Starski). *Class Struggle in Classless Poland*, New York: South End Press, 1982.

Majewska, Ewa. *Kontrpubliczności ludowe i feministyczne. Wczesna Solidarność i Czarne Protesty*, Warszawa: Instytut Wydawniczy Książka i Prasa, 2018.

_____. "Feminist Art of Failure, Ewa Partum and the Weak Avant-Garde," *Widok: A Journal of Visual Culture* 16, 2016.

_____. "La Mestiza from Ukraine?," *Signs: Journal of Women in Culture and Society* 37: 1, 2011.

_____. "Peripheries, Housewives and Artists in Revolt: Notes from the Former East," in S. Sheikh and M. Hlavajova (eds.), *Former West: Art and the Contemporary after 1989*, Cambridge: MIT Press, 2016.

_____. "The Utopia of 'Solidarity' Between Public Sphere and Counter-publics: Institutions of the Common Revisited," *Utopian Studies* 29: 2, 2018.

____. "Weak Resistance," *Krisis Journal* 1: 7, 2018.

Majewska, Ewa and Barbara Godlewska-Bujok. "The Power of the Weak, Neoliberal Biopolitics, and Abortion in Poland," publicseminar.org, April 25, 2016.

Majewska, Ewa and Kuba Szreder. "So Far, So Good: Contemporary Fascism, Weak Resistance, and Postartistic Practices in Today's Poland," *e-flux Journal* 76, 2016.

Malabou, Catherine. *Changing Difference: The Feminine and the Question of Philosophy*, Cambridge: Polity Press, 2011.

Marx, Karl. *Capital: A Critique of Political Economy*, Vol. 1 (1867), London: Penguin, 1990.

____. "List do L. Feuerbacha z 11 sierpnia 1844," in K. Marx and F. Engels, *Dzieła zebrane* vol. 1. Warszawa: Książka i Wiedza, 1960.

Matynia, Elżbieta. "The Lost Treasure of Solidarity," *Social Research* 68: 4, 2001.

Mbembe, Achille. "Necropolitics," transl. L. Meintjes, *Public Culture* 15: 1, 2003.

McLuhan, Marshall. *Understanding Media: The Extensions of Man*, Cambridge: MIT Press, 1994.

Mendes, Kaitlynn, Jessica Ringrose and Jessalynn Keller. "#MeToo and the Promise and Pitfalls of Challenging Rape Culture through Digital Feminist Activism," *European Journal of Women's Studies* 25: 2, 2018.

Michaelis, Loralea. "Rosa Luxemburg on Disappointment and the Politics of Commitment," *European Journal of Political Theory* 10: 2, 2011.

McKee, Yates. *Strike Art*, London: Verso, 2016.

Moore, David. "Is the Post- in Postcolonial the Post- in Post-Soviet? Toward a Global Postcolonial Critique," *PMLA* 116: 1, 2001.

Mouffe, Chantal. "The Radical Centre: A politics without adversary," *Soundings* 9, 1998.

Munck, Ronaldo. "The Precariat: A View from the South," *Third World Quarterly* 34: 5, 2013.

Nagle, Angela. *Kill All Normies: Online Culture Wars from 4chan and Tumblr to Trump and the Alt-Right*, New York: Zero Books, 2017.

Nochlin, Linda. *Women, Art and Power and Other Essays*, New York: Harper & Row, 1988.

Ost, David. *The Defeat of Solidarity: Anger and Politics in Postcommunist Europe*, Ithaca: Cornell University Press, 2005.

____. *Solidarność a polityka antypolityki*, Gdańsk: ECS, 2014.

Pateman, Carole. *The Sexual Contract*, Stanford: Stanford University Press, 1988.

____. *The Disorder of Women*, London: Polity Press, 1989.

Penn, Shana. *Solidarity's Secret: The Women Who Defeated Communism in Poland*, Ann Arbor: University of Michigan Press, 2006.

Peeren, Esther et al. (eds.), *Global Cultures of Contestation: Mobility, Sustainability, Aesthetics and connectivity*, London: Palgrave Macmillan, 2018.

Peters, Sibylle. "On Being Many," in F. Malzacher et al. (eds.), *Truth Is Concrete: A Handbook for Artistic Strategies in Real Politics*, Berlin: Sternberg Press, 2015.

Polan, Dana. "The Public's Fear, or Media as Monster in Habermas, Negt, and Kluge," *Social Text* 25/26, 1990.

Preciado, Paul. *Testo Junkie: Sex, Drugs, and Biopolitics in the Pharmaco-pornographic Era*, transl. B. Benderson, New York: The Feminist Press, 2013.

Rancière, Jacques. *Disagreement: Politics and Philosophy*, transl. J. Rose, Minneapolis: University of Minnesota Press, 2004.

____. *The Emancipated Spectator*, London: Verso, 2010.

____. *Le partage du sensible: Esthétique et politique*, Paris: La Fabrique Editions, 2000.

____. *Proletarian Nights: The Workers' Dream in Nineteenth-Century France*, London: Verso, 2012.

____. *The Philosopher and His Poor*, transl. J. Drury et al., Durham: Duke University Press, 2003.

Raunig, Gerald. *Dividuum: Machinic Capitalism and Molecular Revolution*, Cambridge: MIT Press, 2015.

____. *Factories of Knowledge, Industries of Creativity*, Cambridge: MIT Press, 2013.

____. "Occupy the Theater! Molecularize the Museum! Inventing the (Art) Institution of the Commons," in F. Malzacher (ed.), *Truth Is Concrete: A Handbook for Artistic Strategies in Real Politics*, Berlin: Sternberg Press, 2014.

Reich, Wilhelm. *The Mass Psychology of Fascism*, transl. V. Carfagno, New York: Farrar, Straus & Giroux, 1970.

Riabczuk, Mykola. *Ukraina: Syndrom postkolonialny*, Wrocław-Wojnowice: KEW, 2015.

Rich, Adrienne. *Blood, Bread and Poetry: Selected Prose 1979–1985*, New York: W.W. Norton & Company, 1986.

Ruda, Frank. *Hegel's Rabble: An Investigation into Hegel's Philosophy of Right*, London: Bloomsbury, 2011.

Rudnicki, Cezary. "Jeśli mówić prawdę, to tylko w Sierpniu. Etyka jako polityka," *Praktyka Teoretyczna* 4: 22, 2016.

Ryszka, Franciszek. *Państwo stanu wyjątkowego: rzecz o systemie państwa i prawa Trzeciej Rzeszy*, Wrocław: Zakład Narodowy im. Ossolińskich, 1974.

Scholette, Gregory. *Dark Matter: Art and Politics in the Age of Enterprise Culture*, London: Pluto Press, 2011.

Schradie, Jen. *The Revolution That Wasn't: How Digital Activism Favors Conservatives*, Cambridge: Harvard University Press, 2019.

Scott, James. *Weapons of the Weak: Everyday Forms of Peasant Resistance*, New Haven: Yale University Press, 1986.

Showalter, Elaine. "Representing Ophelia: Women, Madness, and the Responsibilities of Feminist Criticism," in P. Parker and G. Hartman (eds.), *Shakespeare and the Question of Theory*, New York: Methuen, 1985.

Siemieniako, Beata. *Reprywatyzując Polskę. Historia wielkiego przekrętu*, Warszawa: Wydawnictwo Krytyki Politycznej, 2017.

Sontag, Susan. "Waiting for Godot in Sarajevo," *Performing Arts Journal* 16: 2, 1994.

Sowa, Jan. *Inna Rzeczpospolita jest możliwa. Widma przeszłości, wizje przyszłości*, Warszawa: Wydawnictwo WAB, 2015.

Spivak, Gayatri Chakravorty. *A Critique of Postcolonial Reason*, Cambridge: Harvard University Press, 1999.

_____. "Can the Subaltern Speak?" in C. Nelson and L. Grossberg (eds.), *Marxism and the Interpretation of Culture*, Urbana: University of Illinois Press, 1988.

Standing, Guy. *The Precariat: The New Dangerous Class*, London: Bloomsbury Academic, 2011.

Staniszkis, Jadwiga. *Poland's Self-Limiting Revolution,* transl. Jan Gross, Princeton: Princeton University Press, 1984.

Szadkowski, Krystian. *Uniwersytet jako dobro wspólne,* Warszawa: PWN, 2015.

Tarasiewicz, Małgorzata. *Co wy, drogie koleżanki, tak się dajecie?* Published March 8, 2014, KrytykaPolityczna.pl.

Terlecki, Ryszard. *Miecz i tarcza komunizmu. Historia aparatu bezpieczeństwa w Polsce 1944–1990,* Kraków: Wydawnictwo Literackie, 2007.

Theweleit, Klaus. *Male Fantasies,* vol. 1 and 2, Minneapolis: University of Minnesota Press, 1989.

Tiqqun, *Preliminary Materials for a Theory of the Young-Girl.* Cambridge: MIT Press, 2012.

Vattimo, Gianni and Pier Aldo Rovatti (eds.). *Dialectics, Difference, Weak Thought,* New York: SUNY Press, 2012.

Wallerstein, Immanuel. "Semi-peripheral Countries and the Contemporary World Crisis," *Theory and Society* 3: 4, 1976.

Warner, Michael. "Publics and Counterpublics," *Public Culture* 14: 1, 2002.

_____. *Publics and Counterpublics,* New York: Zone Books, 2005.

Wielgosz, Przemysław. "Od zacofania i spowrotem. Wprowadzenie do ekonomii politycznej peryferyjnego miasta przemysłowego," in M. Kaltwasser, E. Majewska, K. Szreder (eds.), *Futuryzm miast przemysłowych,* Kraków: Korporacja Ha! Art, 2007.

Wiśniewska, Agnieszka. *Duża Solidarność, mała solidarność. Biografia Henryki Krzywonos,* Warszawa: Wydawnictwo Krytyki Politycznej, 2010.

Wollny, Zorka (ed.), *Ofelia. Ikonografie Szaleństwa,* Łódź: Muzeum Sztuki, 2018.

Žižek, Slavoj. *Enjoy your Symptom!,* London: Routledge, 1991.

_____. *The Sublime Object of Ideology,* London: Verso, 1989.

_____. *Less Than Nothing: Hegel and the Shadow of Dialectical Materialism,* London: Verso, 2012.

Notes

Introduction: Why Should We Reclaim the Public?

1. I. Wallerstein, "Semi-peripheral Countries and the Contemporary World Crisis," *Theory and Society* 3: 4, 1976.
2. A. Rich, "Notes Towards a Politics of Location," in *Blood, Bread and Poetry: Selected Prose 1979–1985,* New York: W.W. Norton & Company, 1986, 221.
3. See A. Kluge and O. Negt, *Public Sphere and Experience: Analysis of the Bourgeois and Proletarian Public Sphere,* transl. P. Labanyi et al., London: Verso, 2016; Hardt and Negri, *Commonwealth*; M. Hardt and A. Negri, *Assembly,* Oxford: Oxford University Press, 2017; N. Fraser, "Rethinking the Public Sphere: A Contribution to the Critique of Actually Existing Democracy," *Social Text* 25/26, 1990.
4. See G. Raunig, "Occupy the Theater! Molecularize the Museum! Inventing the (Art) Institution of the Commons," in F. Malzacher et al. (eds.), *Truth Is Concrete: A Handbook for Artistic Strategies in Real Politics,* Berlin: Steinberg Press, 2014.
5. These plans, still available in the city's archives, constitute a base for one of the most amazing artworks—the Wartopia project by Warsaw-based artist Aleksandra Polisiewicz, *Wartopia* (2006–).
6. See J. Kusiak, "Legal Technologies of Primitive Accumulation: Judicial Robbery and Dispossession-by-Restitution in Warsaw," *International Journal of Urban and Regional Research* 43: 4 2019. This topic has also been discussed in the book written by one of the most engaged lawyers to help families threatened by evictions, See B. Siemieniako, *Reprywatyzując Polskę. Historia wielkiego przekrętu,* Warszawa: Wydawnictwo Krytyki Politycznej, 2017.

7. B. Geremek, *The Margins of Society in Late Medieval Paris*, Cambridge: Cambridge University Press, 2006; S. Federici, *Caliban and the Witch*, New York: Autonomedia, 2004.

8. D. Ost, *The Defeat of Solidarity: Anger and Politics in Postcommunist Europe*, Ithaca: Cornell University Press, 2005.

9. b. hooks, *Feminist Theory: From Margin to Center*, London: Pluto Press, 2000.

10. H. Lefebvre, "The Right to the City," in E. Kofman and E. Lebas (eds.), *Writings on Cities*, Cambridge: Wiley-Blackwell, 1996.

11. An exhibition curated by Łukasz Ronduda, Szymon Maliborski and Zofia Krawiec, "140 Beats per Minute: Rave Culture and Contemporary Art in 1990s Poland" at the Museum of Modern Art in Warsaw, in summer 2017, was where I saw the first photographs of the events.

12. See Tariq Ali, *The Radical Center*, London: Verso, 2015; Chantal Mouffe, "The Radical Centre: A Politics Without Adversary," *Soundings* 9, 1998.

13. For the notion of necropolitics, see further in this book. The notion comes from: A. Mbembe, "Necropolitics," transl. L. Meintjes, *Public Culture* 15: 1, 2003.

14. See C. Schmitt, *Theory of the Partisan: Intermediate Commentary on the Concept of the Political*, New York: Telos Press 2007; G. Agamben, *State of Exception*, transl. K. Atell, Chicago: University of Chicago Press, 2005; F. Ryszka, *Państwo Stanu wyjątkowego*, Wrocław: Ossolineum, 1973; and E. Majewska, *Feminizm jako filozofia społeczna. Szkice z teorii rodziny*, Warszawa: Difin, 2009.

15. See G. Agamben, *The State of Exception*, transl. K. Atell, Chicago: University of Chicago Press, 2005; F. Ryszka, *Państwo stanu wyjątkowego: rzecz o systemie państwa i prawa Trzeciej Rzeszy*, Wrocław: Zakład Narodowy im. Ossolińskich, 1974.

16. See W. Benjamin, "On the Concept of History," in W. Benjamin, *Selected Writings*, vol. 4, transl. E. Jephcott, Cambridge: Harvard University Press, 2003.

17. See J. Derrida, *Specters of Marx*, London: Routledge, 1993; G. Vattimo, "Weak Thought," in Gianni Vattimo and Pier Aldo Rovatti (eds.), *Weak Thought*, New York: SUNY Press, 2012. See also: E. Majewska, "Feminist Art of Failure, Ewa Partum and the Weak Avant-Garde," *Widok: A Journal of Visual Culture* 16, 2016 and E. Majewska, "Peripheries,

Housewives and Artists in Revolt: Notes from the Former East," in Simon Sheikh and Maria Hlavajova (eds.), *Former West: Art and the Contemporary after 1989*, Cambridge: MIT Press, 2016.

18. L. Michaelis, "Rosa Luxemburg on Disappointment and the Politics of Commitment," *European Journal of Political Theory* 10: 2, 2011.

19. C. Pateman, *The Sexual Contract*, Stanford: Stanford University Press, 1988.

20. See E. Majewska, *Report on Domestic Violence against Women*, published by Amnesty International Poland in 2006; the numbers concerning Sweden were acquired during the study visit I made in the process of writing the report.

1 Revisiting "Solidarity": Counterpublics, Utopia and the Common

1. As a starting point for this chapter, I used the article: E. Majewska, "The Utopia of 'Solidarity' between the Public Sphere and Counterpublics: Institutions of the Common Revisited," *Utopian Studies* 28: 2, 2018.

2. J. Butler, *Notes Toward a Performative Theory of Assembly*, Cambridge: Harvard University Press, 2015.

3. See M. Warner, *Publics and Counterpublics*, New York: Zone Books, 2005.

4. See Kluge and Negt, *Public Sphere and Experience*.

5. The accounts of Solidarność have been numerous and I will only directly reference some of them. Although they provide an enormous amount of information, most of them share a tendency to exclude or marginalize women and the working class, which I would openly contradict in this book; namely, their authors clearly prioritize the agency of the intelligentsia (particularly the members of KOR) for the political strategy of Solidarność. Among the exceptions to this tendency, I should mention: R. Laba, *The Roots of Solidarity: A Political Sociology of Poland's Working-Class Democratization*, Princeton: Princeton University Press, 1991 and J. Sowa, *Inna Rzeczpospolita jest możliwa. Widma przeszłości, wizje przyszłości*, Warszawa: Wydawnictwo WAB, 2015. The work of professor Andrzej Friszke is a prominent example of attributing Solidarność almost solely to the intellectual agency of the Polish oppositional intelligentsia,

See A. Friszke, *Opozycja polityczna w PRL 1945–1980,* London: Wydawnictwo Aneks, 1994; A. Friszke, *Przystosowanie i opór. Studia z dziejów PRL,* Warszawa: Towarzystwo "Więź," 2007 and A. Friszke (ed.), *Solidarność 1980–81 od wewnątrz,* Warszawa: IPN, 2013. Other important works on Solidarność include: T. Garton Ash, *The Polish Revolution: Solidarity,* London: Granta Books and Penguin, 1991; D. Ost, *Solidarność a polityka antypolityki,* Gdańsk: ECS, 2014; J. Staniszkis, *Poland's Self-Limiting Revolution,* transl. Jan Gross, Princeton: Princeton University Press, 1984; J. Kuisz, *Charakter prawny Porozumień Sierpniowych 1980–81,* Warszawa: Fundacja Uniwersytetu Warszawskiego, ECS, Wydawnictwo TRIO, 2009; J. Holzer, *Solidarność 1980–81. Geneza i historia,* Warszawa: Wydawnictwo Krąg, 1984; S. Magala, (S. Starski), *Class Struggle in Classless Poland,* Boston: South End Press, 1982 and S. Kowalski, *Krytyka solidarnościowego rozumu,* Warszawa: Wydawnictwa Akademickie i Profesjonalne, 2009. There is only one woman in this collection, which is striking.

6. Ost, *The Defeat of Solidarity.*

7. Staniszkis, *Poland's Self-Limiting Revolution.*

8. L. Berlant, *Cruel Optimism,* Durham: Duke University Press, 2011.

9. Berlant, *Cruel Optimism,* 2.

10. Ost, *The Defeat of Solidarity.*

11. E. Matynia, "The Lost Treasure of Solidarity," *Social Research* 4: 68, 2001.

12. B. Baczko, *Wyobrażenia społeczne. Szkice o nadziei i pamięci zbiorowej,* Warszawa: PWN, 1994, 96.

13. See Kluge and Negt, *Public Sphere and Experience,* and Habermas, *The Structural Transformation of the Public Sphere,* transl. T. Burger, Cambridge: MIT Press, 1989.

14. E. Bloch, *The Utopian Function of Art and Literature: Selected Essays,* transl. Jack Zipes and Frank Mecklenberg, Cambridge: MIT Press, 1988.

15. Bloch, *The Utopian Function of Art and Literature,* 10.

16. R. Terlecki, *Miecz i tarcza komunizmu. Historia aparatu bezpieczeństwa w Polsce 1944–1990,* Kraków: Wydawnictwo Literackie, 2007, 257.

17. Laba, *The Roots of Solidarity.*

18. Baczko, *Wyobrażenia społeczne,* 87.

19. Baczko, *Wyobrażenia społeczne,* 89.

20. The Gdańsk twenty-one demands read as follows (with some abbreviations, translation from Wikipedia slightly modified by the author, EM): 1. Acceptance of free trade unions independent of the Communist Party and of enterprises . . . 2. A guarantee of the right to strike and of the security of strikers. 3. Compliance with the constitutional guarantee of freedom of speech, the press and publication . . . 4. A return of former rights to: 1) People dismissed from work after the 1970 and 1976 strikes. 2) Students expelled because of their political views. The release of all political prisoners . . . 5. Availability to the mass media of information about the formation of the Inter-factory Strike Committee and publication of its demands. 6. Bringing the country out of its crisis situation by the following means: a) making public complete information about the social-economic situation. b) enabling all social classes to take part in discussion of the reform program. 7. Financial compensation for all workers taking part in the strike for the period of the strike. 8. An increase in the pay of each worker by 2,000 złoty a month. 9. Guaranteed automatic increases in pay on the basis of increases in prices and the decline in real income. 10. A full supply of food products for the domestic market, with exports limited to surpluses. 11. The introduction of food coupons for meat and meat products (until the market stabilizes). 12. The abolition of commercial prices and sales for Western currencies in the so-called internal export companies. 13. Selection of management personnel on the basis of qualifications, not party membership, and elimination of privileges for the state police, security service, and party apparatus by equalization of family allowances and elimination of special sales, etc. 14. Reduction in the age of retirement for women to fifty and for men to fifty-five, or (regardless of age) after working for 30 years (for women) or thirty-five years (for men). 15. Conformity of old-age pensions and annuities with what has actually been paid in. 16. Improvements in the working conditions of the health service. 17. Assurances of a reasonable number of places in day-care centers and kindergartens for the children of working mothers. 18. Paid maternity leave for three years. 19. A decrease in the waiting period for apartments. 20. An increase in the commuter's allowance to 100 złoty. 21. Free Saturdays.

21. Demands of the Elbląg Factory of Repair of the Mechanical Equipment, recollected on January 8, 1971; see the documents collected on the website

of the IPN (National Institute of Rememberance): grudzien70.ipn. gov.pl.

22. M. Foucault, "Of Other Spaces: Utopias and Heterotopias," transl. J. Miskowiec, *Architecture, Mouvement, Continuité* 5, 1984.

23. Z. Kowalewski, *Rendez-nous nos Usines! Solidarnosc dans le combat pour l'autogestion ouvrière*, Montreuil: Presse Éd. Communication, 1985.

24. See Magala, *Class in Classless Poland*.

25. See Staniszkis, *Poland's Self-Limiting Revolution*.

26. A very interesting yet somewhat inconclusive recapitulation of the discussions concerning the legal status of the August Agreements, and thus also Solidarność, can be found in Kuisz, *Charakter prawny Porozumień Sierpniowych 1980–1981*.

27. See Habermas, *The Structural Transformation of the Public Sphere*.

28. See C. Calhoun (ed.), *Habermas and the Public Sphere*, Cambridge: MIT Press, 1992.

29. W. Montag, "The Pressure of the Streets: Habermas's Fear of the Masses," in M. Hill and W. Montag (eds.), *Masses, Classes and the Public Sphere*, London: Verso, 2000.

30. See M. Warner, *Publics and Counterpublics*, New York: Zone Books, 2005.

31. See Kluge and Negt, *Public Sphere and Experience*.

32. Habermas, *The Structural Transformation of the Public Sphere*, 3.

33. Kluge and Negt, *Public Sphere and Experience*, 4.

34. See W. Benjamin, "The Task of Translator," in Benjamin, *Selected Writings, 1: 1913–1926*, Cambridge: Harvard University Press, 1996, 257.

35. Matynia, "The Lost Treasure of Solidarity," 925.

36. See Pateman, *The Sexual Contract*.

37. Henryka Krzywonos was depicted in detail in a biography; see A. Wiśniewska, *Duża Solidarność, mała solidarność. Biografia Henryki Krzywonos*, Warszawa: Wydawnictwo Krytyki Politycznej, 2010. Other monographs depicting women active in Solidarność include: S. Penn, *Solidarity's Secret: The Women Who Defeated Communism in Poland*, Ann Arbor: University of Michigan Press, 2006; M. Dzido, *Kobiety Solidarności*. Warszawa: Świat Książki, 2016 and E. Kondratowicz, *Szminka na sztandarze. Kobiety Solidarności 1980–1989*. Warszawa: Wydawnictwo Sic!, 2001.

38. Sowa, *Inna Rzeczpospolita jest możliwa*.

39. Habermas, *The Structural Transformation of the Public Sphere*, xviii.

40. G. Eley, "Nations, Publics and Political Cultures: Placing Habermas in the Nineteenth Century," in C. Calhoun (ed.), *Habermas and the Public Sphere*, 304.

41. Kluge and Negt, *Public Sphere and Experience*, 7.

42. A. Kluge and O. Negt, *History and Obstinacy*, transl. Richard Langston et al., New York: Zone Books, 2014.

43. Kluge and Negt, *Public Sphere and Experience*, 1.

44. F. Jameson, "On Negt and Kluge," *October* 46, 1988 and D. Polan, "The Public's Fear, or Media as Monster in Habermas, Negt, and Kluge," *Social Text* 25/26, 1990.

45. F. Guattari, *The Three Ecologies*, transl. I. Pindar and P. Sutton, London and Brunschwick: Athlone Press, 2000.

46. See Matynia, "The Lost Treasure of Solidarity" and Sowa, *Inna Rzeczpospolita jest możliwa*.

47. See Sowa, *Inna Rzeczpospolita jest możliwa*, Chapter II.

48. Negri and Hardt, *Commonwealth*, 177.

49. Negri and Hardt, *Commonwealth*, 177.

50. See Negri and Hardt, *Commonwealth*.

51. Laba, *The Roots of Solidarity*.

52. See Friszke, *Opozycja w PRL w latach 1945–1980*.

53. Hardt and Negri, *Assembly*.

54. J. Rancière, *Proletarian Nights: The Workers' Dream in Nineteenth-Century France*, London: Verso, 2012, and J. Rancière, *The Philosopher and His Poor*, transl. J. Drury et al., Durham: Duke University Press, 2003.

55. See G. Spivak, "History," in *A Critique of Postcolonial Reason*, Cambridge: Harvard University Press, 1999.

56. See S. Danius, S. Jonsson and G. Chakravorty Spivak, "An Interview with Gayatri Chakravorty Spivak," *boundary* 2, 20: 2, 1993.

57. E. Dunn, *Privatizing Poland: Baby Food, Big Business, and the Remaking of Labor*, New York: Cornell University Press, 2004.

58. Only one of these books is available in English, see Penn, *Solidarity's Secret*.

59. See Penn, *Solidarity's Secret* and Kondratowicz, *Szminka na sztandarze*.

60. For different notions of the public sphere, see J. Habermas, *The Structural Transformation of the Public Sphere*.

61. M. Dalla Costa and S. James, *Women and the Subversion of the Community/A Woman's Place*, London: Butler and Tanner Ltd., 1972. See also: S. Federici, "Precarious Labor: A Feminist Viewpoint," in *Journal of Aesthetics and Protest Press*, 2008.

62. A. Jónasdóttir, *Love Power and Political Interests*, Örebro: Örebro University Press, 1991.

63. J. Rancière, *Le partage du sensible: Esthétique et politique*, Paris: La Fabrique Editions, 2000.

64. Małgorzata Tarasiewicz, *Co wy, drogie koleżanki, tak się dajecie?* Published March 8, 2014, KrytykaPolityczna.pl.

65. See L. Berlant, *Cruel Optimism*, Durham: Duke University Press, 2011.

2 Feminist Counterpublics: From Ophelia to Current Women's Protests

1. This chapter expands the arguments from two pieces published earlier: E. Majewska, *Ophelic Counterpublics*, in: Z. Wollny (ed.), *Ofelia. Ikonografie Szaleństwa*, Łódź: Muzeum Sztuki, 2018 and E. Majewska, "Feminism will not be televised," *e-flux Journal*, 6: 92, 2018.

2. The piece was staged in the Museum of Art in Łódź (MS Łódź) in 2012. A piece of the documentation of this staging is available at zorkawollny.net/OFELIE.

3. B. Honig, *Antigone, Interrupted*, Cambridge: Cambridge University Press, 2013.

4. K. Marx, *Capital: A Critique of Political Economy*, Vol. 1 (1867), London: Penguin, 1990, 875.

5. C. Pateman, *The Disorder of Women*, London: Polity Press, 1989.

6. H. Cixous, "The Laugh of the Medusa," transl. K. Cohen and P. Cohen, *Signs: Journal of Women in Culture and Society*, 1: 4, 1976, 876.

7. See "Can the Subaltern Speak?" in C. Nelson, L. Grossberg (eds.), *Marxism and the Interpretation of Culture*, Urbana: University of Illinois Press, 1988.

8. E. Showalter, "Representing Ophelia: Women, Madness, and the Responsibilities of Feminist Criticism," in P. Parker, G. Hartman (eds.), *Shakespeare and the Question of Theory*, New York: Methuen, 1985, 77.

9. L. Nochlin, "Why Have There Been No Great Women Artists?" in *Women, Art and Power and Other Essays,* New York: Harper & Row, 1988.

10. Fraser, "Rethinking the Public Sphere."

11. Fraser, "Rethinking the Public Sphere," 57.

12. This point was brilliantly explained and challenged in R. Deutsche, "Art and Public Space: Questions of Democracy," *Social Text* 33, 1992.

13. See Fraser, "Rethinking the Public Sphere."

14. Fraser, "Rethinking the Public Sphere," 73.

15. See Guattari, *Three Ecologies.*

16. For the details of the Women's Strike in Iceland in 1975, See Íris Ellenberger, "The Day Women Brought Iceland to a Standstill," *Jacobin,* October 24, 2019, jacobinmag.com.

17. I discussed the situation in Poland in an interview for *Jacobin,* published at jacobinmag.com in April 2016.

18. This statement was announced in the official dispatch of the Polish Press Agency (Polska Agencja Prasowa, PAP) on October 12, 2016; I quote after the portal tvn24.pl.

19. Mbembe, "Necropolitics," 11.

20. There are several important analyses of the Nazi ideology of antisemitism; for me, the most important are those combining antisemitism and sexism in the fascist political doctrine, thus proving the structural intertwining of the two hate speeches. See, for example, W. Reich, *The Mass Psychology of Fascism,* transl. V. Carfagno, New York: Farrar, Straus & Giroux, 1970 and K. Theweleit, *Male Fantasies,* Minneapolis: University of Minnesota Press, 1989.

21. See Theweleit, *Male Fantasies.*

22. J. Butler and G. Spivak, *Who Sings the Nation-State?: Language, Politics, Belonging,* London: Seagull, 2011. See also: E. Majewska, "La Mestiza from Ukraine? Border Crossing with Gloria Anzaldúa," *Signs* 37: 1, 2011.

23. See Pateman, *The Sexual Contract*; J. Herman, *Trauma and Recovery: The Aftermath of Violence—from Domestic Abuse to Political Terror,* New York: Basic Books, 1992 and A. Honneth, *The Struggle for Recognition,* Cambridge: MIT Press, 1996.

24. See A. Graff and E. Korolczuk, "Gender as 'Ebola from Brussels': The Anti-colonial Frame and the Rise of Illiberal Populism," *Signs: Journal of Women in Culture and Society* 4: 43, 2018.

25. A longer description of the "gender wars" in Poland can be found in E. Korolczuk, "'The War on Gender' from a Transnational Perspective—Lessons for Feminist Strategising," published in 2017, pl.boell.org.

26. For a concise description of the "gender wars," see E. Korolczuk, "'The War on Gender' from a Transnational Perspective."

27. I discuss the protests and their causes in several texts, including: E. Majewska, "When Polish Women Revolted," *Jacobin*, March 3, 2018, and E. Majewska and B. Godlewska-Bujok, "The Power of the Weak, Neoliberal Biopolitics, and Abortion in Poland," April 25, 2016, PublicSeminar.org.

28. T. Bhattacharya, "Mapping Social Reproduction Theory," February 15, 2018, Versobooks.com.

29. "Polityka w sieci, 2016," report published October 2016, politykawsieci.pl/.

30. J. Jaworska, "Moda żałobna przed wybuchem powstania styczniowego," *Przegląd Humanistyczny* 57/1: 436, 2013.

31. For information on the International Women's Strike, see parodemujeres.com.

32. Written in October 2018.

33. Fraser, "Rethinking the Public Sphere."

34. See J. Butler, *Gender Trouble: Feminism and the Subversion of Identity*, New York: Routledge, 1990.

35. See Cixous, "The Laugh of the Medusa" and the interview I conducted with Cixous, "Od *Śmiechu Meduzy* do rynku wojny. An Interview," *Lewą Nogą* 16, 2004.

36. The action has been extensively described in "The Woman Who Created #MeToo Long Before Hashtags," *New York Times*, October 20, 2017.

37. See K. Mendes, J. Ringrose and J. Keller, "#MeToo and the promise and pitfalls of challenging rape culture through digital feminist activism," *European Journal of Women's Studies* 2: 25, 2018. I am grateful to Elżbieta Korolczuk for discussing her research on the media and feminism with me and for sharing some of her resources. See also: T. Bhattacharia, "Socializing Security, Unionizing Work," in *Where Freedom Starts: Sex, Power, Violence, #Metoo*, London: Verso, 2017.

38. L. Berlant, "The Subject of True Feeling," in A. Sarat and T. Kearns (eds.), *Cultural Pluralism, Identity Politics, and the Law*, Ann Arbor: University of Michigan Press, 1999.

39. See Honig, *Antigone, Interrupted*, 182–3, emphasis in original.

40. Among different feminist critiques of such faulty representation of all

women by a small group (of white, upper-class US feminists), the one I tend to appreciate for its focus on solidarity is that offered in: b. hooks, *Feminist Theory: From Margin to Center*, London: Pluto Press, 1990.

41. See C. Malabou, *Changing Difference: The Feminine and the Question of Philosophy*, Cambridge: Polity Press, 2011, 140.

42. S. Ahmed, *Willful Subjects*, Durham: Duke University Press, 2014.

43. Ahmed, *Willful Subjects*, 4.

44. K. Szadkowski, *Uniwersytet jako dobro wspólne*, Warszawa: PWN, 2015.

45. See A. Davis, G. Chakravorty Spivak and N. Dhawan, "Planetary Utopias," *Radical Philosophy* 2: 5, 2019.

46. M. Douglas, *How Institutions Think*, New York: Syracuse University Press, 1986.

47. For a great discussion of Rosa Luxemburg and the issue of failure, see Loralea Michaelis, "Rosa Luxemburg on Disappointment and the Politics of Commitment."

48. In the argument about rehearsal, my work is indebted and inspired by this short yet very interesting essay: S. Peters, "On Being Many," in F. Malzacher (ed.), *Truth is Concrete*.

49. N. Fraser, "How Feminism Became Capitalism's Handmaiden and How to Reclaim It," *Guardian*, October 14, 2013.

50. The gender inequality within precarized societies has been studied by several feminist scholars, including: L. Fantone, "Precarious Changes: Gender and Generational Politics in Contemporary Italy," *Feminist Review* 87: 1, 2007, and S. Federici, "Precarious Labor: A Feminist Viewpoint." The experience of precarity differently influences individuals depending on their ethnic and geopolitical origins, see R. Munck, "The Precariat: a view from the South," *Third World Quarterly* 34: 5, 2013. See also E. Majewska, "Prekariat i dziewczyna. W stronę feministycznej krytyki ekonomii politycznej," *Praktyka Teoretyczna* 1: 15, 2015.

51. See E. Dunn, *The Privatization of Poland*.

52. B. Lipton, "Gender and Precarity: A Response to Simon During," *Australian Humanities Review* 58, 2015, 64.

53. The rejection of compromise became the theme of a feminist action in Poznań carried out in 2017 by Zofia Holeczek, Marta Szymanowska and Joanna Zioła. A clip can be seen on YouTube: "#DOŚĆKOMPROMISÓW— Manifa Poznań / 5.03.2017."

54. For the common, See Hardt and Negri, *Commonwealth* and Raunig, "Occupy the Theater, Molecularize the Museum!"

3 Counterpublics of the Common in Communication Capitalism

1. Hardt and Negri, *Commonwealth*, viii.
2. Hardt and Negri, *Assembly*, 223.
3. See Hardt and Negri, *Assembly*, 240 and following.
4. See Hardt and Negri, *Assembly*, 256.
5. Hardt and Negri, *Assembly*, 254 and following.
6. Hardt and Negri, *Assembly*, 257.
7. Hardt and Negri, *Assembly*, 257.
8. Hardt and Negri, *Assembly*, 41.
9. See J. Dean and P. Passavant, *The Empire's New Clothes*, New York: Routledge, 2004 and further in this chapter.
10. See Guattari, *The Three Ecologies*.
11. See Spivak, "Can the Subaltern Speak?" in *Marxism and the Interpretation of Culture*, in C. Nelson, L. Grossberg (eds.), Urbana: University of Illinois Press, 1988.
12. See Negri and Hardt, *Multitude*; F. Ruda, *Hegel's Rabble: An Investigation into Hegel's Philosophy of Right*, London: Bloomsbury, 2011, and W. Benjamin, "On the Concept of History."
13. See G. Raunig, *Dividuum: Machinic Capitalism and Molecular Revolution*, Cambridge: MIT Press, 2015, and Raunig, "Occupy the Theater."
14. Raunig, *Dividuum*, 67.
15. Raunig, "Occupy the Theater," 76.
16. Hardt and Negri, *Assembly*, 257–78.
17. Kluge and Negt, *Public Sphere and Experience*.
18. See J. Rancière, *Disagreement: Politics and Philosophy*, transl. J. Rose, Minneapolis: University of Minnesota Press, 2004, and S. Žižek, *The Sublime Object of Ideology*, London: Verso, 1989.
19. P. Preciado, *Testo Junkie: Sex, Drugs, and Biopolitics in the Pharmacopornographic Era*, transl. B. Benderson, New York: Feminist Press, 2013, 49.

20. See A. Kluge and O. Negt, *History and Obstinacy*, transl. R. Langston (et al.), New York: Zone Books, 2014.

21. This observation concerning the role of "examples" in Hegel's work appears in Žižek's books and lectures—for example, in his presentation at NYU on November 9, 2016.

22. T. Adorno and M. Horkheimer, *The Dialectic of Enlightenment*, transl. E. Jephcott, Stanford: Stanford University Press, 2002.

23. M. McLuhan, *Understanding Media: The Extensions of Man*, Cambridge: MIT Press, 1994.

24. S. Hall, "Encoding, Decoding," in S. During (ed.), *The Media Studies Reader*, New York: Routledge, 1993.

25. Hall, "Encoding, Decoding," 93.

26. See also J. Halberstam, *The Queer Art of Failure*, Durham: Duke University Press, 2010 and N. Klein, *No Logo: Taking Aim at the Brand Bullies*, London: Picador and Random House, 1999.

27. J. Rancière, *The Emancipated Spectator*, London: Verso, 2010.

28. Polan, "The Public's Fear," 262.

29. See Jameson, "On Kluge and Negt."

30. Jameson, "On Kluge and Negt," 157.

31. J. Dean, "Why the Net Is Not a Public Sphere," *Constellations* 10: 1, 2003.

32. Dean, "Why the Net Is Not a Public Sphere," 97.

33. Dean, "Why the Net is Not a Public Sphere," 101.

34. A detailed analysis of the "White Town" was offered in J. Kubisa, *Bunt białych czepków*, Warszawa: Wydawnictwo Naukowe Scholar, 2014. I also detail it in a chapter of the collected volume: E. Majewska, "Weak Resistance in Semi-Peripheries."

35. Several scholars and activists tried to discuss the recent cases of art censorship in Poland and the region; see for example, the works of Izabela Kowalczyk, including her blog at strasznasztuka.blox.pl and the online Polish Theatre Journal.

36. Bhattacharia, "Socializing Security, Unionizing Work."

37. See Michaelis, "Rosa Luxemburg on Disappointment and the Politics of Commitment."

38. K.J. Lopez, M.L. Muldoon and J.K.L. McKeown, "One Day of #Feminism: Twitter as a Complex Digital Arena for Wielding, Shielding, and Trolling Talk on Feminism," *Leisure Sciences: An Interdisciplinary Journal* 41: 4, 2018.

39. A. Nagle, *Kill All Normies: Online Culture Wars from 4chan and Tumblr to Trump and the Alt-Right*, New York: Zero Books, 2017.

40. J. Schradie, *The Revolution That Wasn't: How Digital Activism Favors Conservatives*, Cambridge: Harvard University Press, 2019.

4 Weak Resistance: Beyond the Heroic Model of Political Agency

1. See Nochlin, "Why have There Been No Great Women Artists?"

2. This notion was first used as the title of the conference "Weak Resistance" at ICI Berlin in 2015, which I co-organized with Rosa Barotsi and Walid al-Houri. In the following years, however, I worked on it in discussion with other scholars, nevertheless mainly on my own. There is a "dictionary definition" available in *Krisis Journal for Contemporary Philosophy*, 2, 2018: a theory of antifascism as weak resistance: Ewa Majewska and Kuba Szreder, "So Far, So Good: Contemporary Fascism, Weak Resistance, and Postartistic Practices in Today's Poland," *e-flux Journal*, 76, 2016, and a longer analysis in my monograph: E. Majewska, *Kontrpubliczności ludowe i feministyczne. Wczesna Solidarność i Czarne Protesty*, Warszawa: IWKIP, 2018.

3. See Benjamin, "On the Philosophy of History," in Vattimo and Rovatti (eds.), *Weak Thought*, and Derrida, *Specters of Marx*. See also S. Khatib, "The Messianic Without Messianism: Walter Benjamin's Materialist Theology," *Anthropology and Materialism* 1, 2013.

4. D. Haraway, "A Cyborg Manifesto," in *Simians, Cyborgs and Women: The Reinvention of Nature*, New York: Routledge, 1991; D. Haraway, "Situated Knowledges: The Science Question in Feminism and the Privilege of Partial Perspective," *Feminist Studies* 3: 14, 1988, and Laboria Cuboniks, "Xenofeminism: A Politics for Alienation," published in several languages in 2015 at laboriacuboniks.net and in print: Laboria Cuboniks, *The Xenofeminist Manifesto*, London: Verso, 2018.

5. D. Haraway, *Staying with the Trouble: Making Kin in the Chthulucene*, Durham: Duke University Press, 2016, 3.

6. For more details on their dispute, see S. Sontag, "Waiting for Godot in Sarajevo," *Performing Arts Journal*, 16: 2, 1994, pp. 87–106 and J. Baudrillard,

"Waiting for Godot, 'No Pity for Sarajevo'"; "The West's Serbianization"; "When the West Stands in for the Dead," in T. Cushman and S.G. Meštrović (eds.), *This Time We Knew: Western Responses to Genocide in Bosnia*, New York: NYU Press, 1996.

7. See J. Baudrillard, *The Gulf War Did Not Take Place*, Bloomington: Indiana University Press, 1995.

8. Sontag, "Waiting for Godot in Sarajevo," 104.

9. J. Scott, *Weapons of the Weak: Everyday Forms of Peasant Resistance*, New Haven: Yale University Press, 1985.

10. This and the next quotation: Scott, *Weapons of the Weak*, xvi.

11. Some parts of this chapter have been presented at ICI Berlin in 2015.

12. Z. Bujak in V. Havel, *Open Letters: Selected Writings 1965–1990*, ed. Paul Wilson, New York: Knopf, 1991, 126.

13. V. Havel, "The Power of the Powerless," *International Journal of Politics* 3/4: 15, 1985–86, 23.

14. Havel, "The Power of the Powerless," 23.

15. Havel, "The Power of the Powerless," 40.

16. Havel, "The Power of the Powerless," 43.

17. Scott, *Weapons of the Weak*.

18. Halberstam, *The Queer Art of Failure*, 2.

19. See Halberstam, *The Queer Art of Failure*, as well as J. Butler, *Gender Trouble*.

20. E. Majewska, "The Common in the Time of Creative Reproductions: On Gerald Raunig's Factories of Knowledge, Industries of Creativity," *e-flux Journal* 5: 62, 2015.

21. See S. Žižek, *Less Than Nothing: Hegel and the Shadow of Dialectical Materialism*, London: Verso, 2012.

22. Michaelis, "Rosa Luxemburg on Disappointment and the Politics of Commitment," 202.

23. In his lectures about the *ritournelle* from 1977, Deleuze emphasized the role of the nonheroic, "Wagner, c'est encore d'un bout à l'autre l'éducation sentimentale. Le héros wagnérien dit: 'Apprenez-moi la peur.' Nietzsche ce n'est pas ça. Il n'y a que des heccéités, c'est-à-dire des combinaisons d'intensités, des composés intensifs. Les heccéités ce ne sont pas des personnes, ce ne sont pas des sujets," in G. Deleuze, "Cours Vincennes: Sur la Musique," March 8, 1977, webdeleuze.com.

24. G. Deleuze and F. Guattari, *Mille Plateaux*, Paris: Editions du Minuit, 1981, 311.

25. Deleuze and Guattari, *Mille Plateaux*.

26. Deleuze and Guattari, *Mille Plateaux*, 342.

27. Deleuze and Guattari, *Mille Plateaux*, 350.

28. Deleuze and Guattari, *Mille Plateaux*, 342.

29. Deleuze and Guattari, *Mille Plateaux*, 4.

30. Raunig, *Factories of Knowledge*, 9.

31. Raunig, *Factories of Knowledge*, 11.

32. See G. Anzaldúa, *Borderlands/La Frontera*, San Francisco: Aunt Lute Books, 1987.

33. Derrida, *Specters of Marx*.

34. See Derrida, *Specters of Marx*, and S. Žižek, *Enjoy your Symptom!* London: Routledge, 1991.

35. M. Riabczuk, *Ukraina. Syndrom postkolonialny*, Wrocław-Wojnowice: KEW, 2015.

36. M. Janion, *Niesamowita słowiańszczyzna*, Kraków: Wydawnictwo Literackie, 2006.

37. D. Moore, "Is the Post- in Postcolonial the Post- in Post-Soviet? Toward a Global Postcolonial Critique," *PMLA* 116: 1, 2001.

38. P. Wielgosz, "Od zacofania i spowrotem. Wprowadzenie do ekonomii politycznej peryferyjnego miasta przemysłowego," in M. Kaltwasser, E. Majewska, K. Szreder (eds.), *Futuryzm miast przemysłowych*, Kraków: Korporacja Ha! Art, 2007.

39. Wallerstein, "Semi-peripheral Countries and the Contemporary World Crisis."

40. See also E. Dunn, *Privatizing Poland* and B. Buden, *O końcu postkomunizmu*, Warszawa: Wydawnictwo Krytyki Politycznej, 2012.

41. Wallerstein, "Semi-peripheral Countries," 462.

42. Wallerstein, "Semi-peripheral Countries," 464.

43. Wallerstein, "Semi-peripheral Countries," 466.

44. Janion, *Niesamowita Słowiańszczyzna*.

45. M. Janion, "List do Uczestników Kongresu Kultury Polskiej," 2016.

46. B. Groys, "Weak Universalism", *e-flux Journal* 15, 2010

47. Majewska, "Feminist Art of Failure, Ewa Partum and the Weak Avant-Garde."

Conclusion: Toward Antifascist Futures

1. See Peters, "On Becoming Many."
2. S. Ahmed, *The Cultural Politics of Emotion*, New York: Routledge, 2004.
3. See Žižek, *Enjoy your Symptom!*
4. K. Marx, "List do L. Feuerbacha z 11 sierpnia 1844," in K. Marx and F. Engels, *Dzieła zebrine*, vol. 1. Warszawa: Książka i Wiedza, [1844] 1960, 642 (translated from Polish by EM, emphasis in the original).
5. See Kuisz, *Charakter prawny porozumień sierpniowych.*
6. See L. Duggan, *The Twilight of Equality? Neoliberalism, Cultural Politics, and the Attack on Democracy,* New York: Beacon Press, 2004.

Index